RETURN

(Re)membering a Family Life

RETURN

(Re)membering a Family Life

Julia Doggart

CRAFTED
ESSENCE
PUBLISHING

ISBN 978-0-9568246-0-8
Published by Crafted Essence Publishing
Cover design by Laurence Fleury

For my mother and father with love

Contents

Letter to Family - *March 2010*

If you are reading this letter, it is because you are a member of my family or someone close to me who features in this book. First, let me thank you for your perfect role in my life and for your willingness or resistance to being in these pages.

It feels fitting that I began printing out my first full draft of this book on March 17th, the anniversary of my father's death. I did not plan it that way, but I am grateful for the feeling it engenders of having completed more than just a book.

As I write this, I am looking out of the bedroom window at my mother's house feeling a sense of calm and, somewhere deeper, the stirrings of whatever comes next. Writing my story has felt grace-filled. It is like accompanying yourself consciously on the journey of your life and saying from time to time, "Ah yes, that feels good. I like it." Perhaps you will be surprised by some of the things you read; perhaps you will not warm to or recognize depictions of yourself or others.

Remember that the story is told from my perspective at different times in my life, and I have tried to recapture the moods and attitudes of earlier times. These are not experiences that hang heavy; these are experiences that have been richly felt, distilled into their greatest value for me, and then allowed to take their chosen and appropriate places in the larger story of my life.

It has felt important to me to write honestly, clearly and with integrity. In doing so, I may have included things in the book that feel exposing or too private for your tastes. I have not done so lightly, and I hope that I have done it well.

Although I have missed not having a father, I believe that he has offered as much through his absence as he might have offered had he lived, just in a different way. I hope that this honors his memory, not through silence or hiding but through telling a story in the most truthful way that I can.

> *Above all, this is a celebration of life with no regret.*
> *With much love and appreciation,*
> *Julia*

PART ONE
LOSS

1

THE SHAPE OF LOSS

Time stood still on March 17, 1965, and I have come home to pry it loose. My father's death stopped time, but like a gathering fault line sent cracks and tremors radiating underground that touched each one of us. His death left grooves and hollows the way water etches itself on stone.

A photograph taken in Cornwall shows us intact, complete, a family of five innocently enjoying a holiday. It is late summer 1964, and we are posed along a wall in the picturesque village of Crackington Haven. Behind us, a car park gives way to scrubland, and sandy paths reach up into low-lying hills. In front, not in the picture, mounds of pebbles undulate to a wide beach and the swell and drag of the tide.

In the centre of the photograph, my mother holds me on her lap. We form a striking contrast – my white dress and blonde curls set against her dark hair and black sweater-top. While I point excitedly at something outside the frame, eyes wide and mouth open to reveal two milk teeth, she smiles directly into the camera with fingers interlaced around my stomach as if I am part of her.

To our right, my father holds three-year-old Richard. They look strained, as if Peter had rushed to take his place for a self-timed shot. He squints and smiles, gripping his fingers around his young son's chest, while Richard stares balefully ahead. A tummy bug and a herd of cows that moo loudly outside his bedroom window have apparently frayed my brother's normally sunny mood. Alone, at the other end of the frame, nine-year-old Michael presses his palms down on the wall and stretches his mouth in a close-lipped smile; he looks as if he has tasted something private and sweet.

I return to this spot in October 2008, touching the wall with inquisitive fingers, as if it held the promise and pain of our family's love. Above me, on the hillside overlooking the bay, the thatched house that my parents rented in 1964 looks unchanged. Its white stucco exterior curves impassively, and the black windows lie closed against the autumn chill. Neither the wall nor the house has registered our loss. It is not indifference so much as a quality of detachment - a consciousness in the landscape that absorbs individual stories and renders personal history somewhat remote. It is against this steady, pulsing presence that I have returned, twenty-six years after leaving England, to trace the particular waves and ridges of our family life. My intention is clear: to know and feel my story in all of its particulars so that I can release the emotional legacy of the past.

My first formal investigations began earlier in 2008, during a two-month visit to my mother's cottage in Lurgashall, West Sussex. As if to prepare the way for my more permanent return that summer, I was dredging the uncertain past for stories that would help reveal and define our family's emotional shape. Over hot spinach and nutmeg soup at the local Noah's Ark pub one damp evening in May, I asked my mother questions about my father that we had covered many times. What kind of man was he? What did he love? How did she meet him?

As she responded to these questions, my mother began confidently enough, treading the central line of her story with firm steps. Then a stray detail would flash in her peripheral vision, and the narrative would scatter like marbles on ice.

"He never liked to post his letters into the red English post-boxes," she told me conspiratorially. "He did not believe that anyone would collect them."

We registered this oddity, and then, as she spread butter on the warm bread accompanying our soup, my mother announced: "Peter adored bread. When we were in a restaurant, he would nudge me to order more when he had barely started what was on his plate."

She smiled at this memory and softened, her faintly lined face almost re-capturing the elasticity of youth. At eighty-six, she seemed able to shift back into the past easily, almost as if she were closing one door in her mind and opening another.

"I was making marmalade once," she continued, "and my mother, Gubby as we called her, kept stirring the pot I had lain aside for cooling, so it wouldn't set. Your father eventually took her by the shoulders and shook her to make her stop."

As she offers these random memories, I piece my father together like a cubist painting where the strangely shaped features do not match. He is a ghostly presence, never quite resurrected, no matter how many stories I hear, and never quite put to rest. He haunts through absence and incompletion, reaching into our lives whenever there is a conduit for loss.

The previous week, we had attended a funeral in the village. The husband of one of my mother's friends had died after an eighteen-month struggle with cancer.

"I am afraid I will be too emotional," my mother had whispered, as she leaned towards me outside the church gates and fidgeted with her gloves. She had already asked several times, as we walked across the village green, if the clothes she was wearing were appropriate. Did the slip go with the skirt? Was the light yellow jacket a good match for the decorative pattern on the rest of her black ensemble?

"Why does it matter if you get emotional?" I had whispered back.

"I have no right; it is not *my* husband who has died," she simply said.

Yet it *is* her husband, dead many years now, always skirting the edges of our lives and pressing into any loss. The emotion lingers, a persistent residue that will not dissolve, as if my father's spirit has not found its rest.

As we entered the churchyard gate and made our way down the narrow stone path, the tidy unassuming graves leaned in to each

5

other for comfort, and the great forked yew bowed its head. The air seemed wrapped in silence, disturbed only by our echoing footsteps and then the creak of the great oak door.

People had not come in droves as expected; the locals, perhaps scared off by the anticipation of a London crowd, had also stayed away, and the church was only a quarter-full. Despite this, my mother chose a seat halfway back on the left, blending interest with her customary unassuming presence. Although she attends church regularly, was raised to it in fact since her father was Rector of a parish in Wales all her young life, my mother is a humble penitent. When she enters a church, something akin to holiness or extreme reverence wraps her small figure in a gentle cocoon of grace. On the rare occasions that I am there, distanced by the mournful condemnation of the prayer book, a glance towards my mother tucked neatly into the choir stalls disarms my resistance and softens my critical edge.

At the funeral, however, she was not in the choir stalls; she was in the body of the church. As the first strains of the organ reverberated and the congregation rose, I felt her stiffen and brace like the victim of an earthquake registering an aftershock. Together, we watched the bereaved family enter the transept slowly - the graceful widow in front, then the daughter, then two sons taut with loss. Separated from us by the structure of the church, their mourning seemed remote and dignified; still, it had touched us.

At the organ's crescendo, the Rector appeared and began to tack down the centre aisle, crisp vestments billowing, until he reached port and started speaking in the strange singsong cadence that swallows words. Behind me, a man asked if his hearing aid was buzzing.

"Not many people here," the man added, while his wife shushed him, and the woman to my right suppressed nervous giggles.

Later, when the Rector had spoken at length about death and resurrection, the same man complained that he was being long-winded. Right on cue, as if he had spoken for the crowd, the congregation murmured, "Amen" precipitously. The Rector paused, punctuating the error, then swept on regardless. Lulled by his excess words, I had not prepared myself for the shock of four men walking forward to pick up the coffin. My chest tightened, as if one chamber had closed shut.

When the men began their sombre walk, dipping gently so the flowers on the coffin cleared the ornate wooden divide, the nave seemed to stretch like a passageway between this life and the next. I tried to picture the body lodged in the narrow shiny box – a vibrant being reduced to cramped quarters where his arms would be pinched and his legs compressed. Although there would be people and stories left behind, a trail of evidence that he had been here, the portal through which this singular man had looked and loved was now closed for good.

When we left the church and made our way back across the village green and down the lane past my mother's cottage to the village hall, the reticence of loss was lubricated by wine. Memories of the deceased floated among the plates of sandwiches, sausage rolls, quiches, and miniature Yorkshire puddings. Only occasionally, whispered complaints about the Rector's loquaciousness filtered through the murmurs of, "Oh, what a lovely service."

Back home, restless and blurred by wine and grief, my mother took solace in her garden. With anxious face upturned towards mine, hand gripping her trowel, she tried to lure me into weeding, digging, or mowing if I preferred something more active. But I resisted her efforts and left the agitated garden for a long walk.

Following a well-trodden way across the football field, I passed the rabbits hidden among the nettles and turned down a leafy path towards a rough wooden bridge. The small stream was almost stagnant – a brown soup clogged with broken branches where stray plastic bags had snagged. In heavy rains, the water could swell to the lip of the bank, turgid and roiling, but it always subsided, sinking back into a slow shallow eddy and becoming, once again, a playground for dogs.

Beyond the bridge, wild bluebells had shared their secrets in a patch of woodland, but now, in early May, the purple traces and viscous stalks were signs of their waning. The wild garlic had taken over - a rampage of lush leaves topped with a storm of delicate white flowers; the scent was dense and smoky.

I walked on, over the fingers and toes of patient oaks, where the land opened up to fields. With footsteps scattering pheasants, I edged the farmers' crops and moved on into denser woods where the leaf canopy arched like the ribs of a mermaid and creepers wound their wily way up trunks. My breath slowed, nature slipped her soft hand in mine, and the weight of the past lifted as birds filled with song.

2

Although it was a dress rehearsal – a two-month interlude that would reveal the knots and grooves of our co-habitation - my mother had shed tears on my arrival. Having measured the time and distance of our separation in years and miles, she knew that a significant chapter of my life had ended. In two months time, when I would return to America in order to collect my dog and more of my belongings, it would be on a tourist visa; America had finally handed me back.

My own feelings about this visit had been less certain. As I left the bright lights of the Chicago airport on May 7th 2008, rather in the manner of a condemned woman, I wondered how I would adjust to the scale and substance of home after the vast and hopeful landscapes of the Midwest. But on the surface at least, my arrival and repatriation had been unremarkable. Accustomed to the questions and fingerprinting of US immigration officials, lined up in cubicles across hard shiny floors, the process of return had seemed benign and simple. British nationals of various shapes and colours had queued along a carpeted hallway and then filed quickly past a cluster of immigration staff seated casually at wooden podiums. In my case, with a mere glance at my passport the young official had acknowledged that I belonged.

I had pushed and bumped my luggage cart through the green zone similarly unmolested, hampered only by one stubbornly stuck wheel, and emerged into the gauntlet of the arrivals' hall. Ahead of me, and on both sides, bodies had surged at the barriers while phlegmatic chauffeurs held up cards with unpronounceable names.

For several long seconds, I had gone unclaimed. Then, a modest figure, clad in khaki trousers and blue linen jacket, had raised one arm among the crowd. It was my brother, Michael, unexpectedly tanned and with a touch more grey in his hair. He greeted me calmly, as if I had just returned from a short trip, and as we left the car park and hurtled into the surrounding countryside, in the nip-and-tuck style he favours, we talked of trivial matters.

It appeared that my body had been quickly absorbed into the mundane activities and the casual intimacies of family life. But on the inside, in my subtle consciousness, the separation between home and self still gaped. Although I had chosen to return, I carried small pockets of resistance heavy with impressions from the past.

My mother's tears on the threshold of home reminded me that intimacy was simpler from a distance. From another continent, I could write long letters or speak on the phone, and at the end of brief visits, I could slip written declarations of love into my mother's purse or under her pillow. Coming home now in a more open-ended way, depending on my mother, inevitably pulled me back to earlier days when the love between us had felt dangerous, too close, as if our emotional wires were easily crossed and tangled.

Just days into my visit, internal tensions had surfaced during a shopping trip to the nearby town of Midhurst. As I steered my mother's small, red Renault through the narrow lanes, throngs of shoppers, and blinking pedestrian lights, she had kept up a constant commentary while surreptitiously watching the speedometer and gripping her seat.

"It's just thirty here, dear, and watch out for that corner. The road gets really narrow."

As we turned into the car park, she had indicated a vacant spot, but I swept past it and drove to the furthest corner where I parked under a weeping willow tree. A teenage boy and girl strolled towards us hand-in-hand. A fresh cut on the girl's upper arm released a thin trickle of blood that stood out vividly against her white skin. I wondered if my mother had noticed, but she said nothing. Perhaps the cut signalled a pact of some kind or gave the girl an edge in the complicated politics of secondary school.

We left the car and walked into town at the pace of old people, Mum in her skirt and soft-soles and me in capris, tie-dyed t-shirt and resilient brown sneakers. We stopped at a delicatessen, a small shop sandwiched between a second-hand bookstore and an opticians, where my mother drew me towards the displays of cheeses, thick-skinned quiches and mounds of fresh pâté.

"Is there anything you want, darling?" she enquired.

I shook my head, and she apologized to the man behind the counter as if we had inconvenienced him. Two doors down, a display of hats in the window of a dress shop caught my mother's attention.

"Your cousin's getting married in September," she said. "I need a new hat for that."

"Don't you already have hats?" I asked, dreading a prolonged session in the boutique that was laden with floral dresses and pleated skirts.

"I don't want him ashamed of his great-aunt," she replied, as she sailed in.

While my mother tried on hats, I pondered the fact that driving her three hundred miles north to the wedding in Durham would probably be one of my duties. Relations I had not seen in years would suddenly be woven back into my life.

"How does this look?" she asked, minutes later, raising her hands towards the silver hat perched on her head like an upside-down acorn.

"It might look better if you take out the filling paper," I replied.

She laughed, and I escaped onto the street just as the heavily made-up shop assistant scanned my mother's five-foot frame and calibrated her voice for an intervention.

"Perhaps a tipped-up brim might be better, madam, since you are not *all* that tall?"

While discussions continued inside, I stood on the pavement and watched small groups of shoppers move up and down the narrow lanes, clutching their re-usable bags and conducting business in a restrained and capable way. It felt so different from the casual opulence of America where shopping was part-entertainment, often made pleasurable by take-away coffee and tasty snacks. There are fewer pleasures here it seemed, or different pleasures that I did not recognize yet.

On the drive back from Midhurst, I was testy with directions, and at dinner, resorted to well-practiced buffering techniques designed to keep my mother at a distance.

"No, I don't want to discuss other members of the family in their absence; no, I can't really offer much detail about my next steps, since I don't have them yet; no, I'd rather not focus on all the depressing news in the country such as money shortages or failed government policies."

"I'm wondering what I *can* talk about," my mother wryly noted.

Her words cut through my defences; for a moment, I let down my guard. But as I spoke of what I was leaving behind – my friends; my car; furniture; a sense of belonging; and, at least temporarily, my dog – she dove into the small opening and filled it with her anxieties and concerns. How would I adapt to living here? Would I be happy? Was it the right move?

"I find your anxiety really difficult," I told her. "Can't you be excited for me, or curious perhaps?"

"It's different when you are a mother," she said, fingering her glass of water and lowering her head. "You just don't understand."

"But isn't anxiety an inner thing? Isn't it something you can regulate?"

"I have lived with it for a lifetime," she declared, her eyes filling with tears.

Two years ago, worried phone calls from my brother, and my mother's neighbours, had sent me rushing back from America, leaving my teaching responsibilities with willing friends.

"Your mother is acting strangely; she's talking way too fast," one neighbour had told me.

"She's getting days and events confused; she isn't eating or sleeping," another neighbour had said.

"I helped her tidy her room, and she muddled it up again," a third neighbour exclaimed, with just a hint of indignation in her voice.

In the days before I rushed home, my mother would often phone in the middle of her night; in fevered tones, she would recall odd details of her life or obsessively read the directions on her medication packets. She was fearful, paranoid about her safety, and endlessly chasing her mind down long corridors or into dead ends.

She was having what was later diagnosed as a "bipolar hyper-manic episode." I prefer to think of it as a massive and simultaneous download of all the thoughts my mother has ever had. They rushed into her mind like a swarm of locusts picking at the structure, feeding on it, and sending her here and there chasing different impulses like a laboratory rat.

When the taxi had deposited me in the driveway two years ago, I had stood there for a moment facing the house and searching for signs of disturbance. And then my mother had suddenly popped her head out of the bedroom window and ducked back down rather in the manner of a child's jack-in-the-box.

The front door had been left open, and as I entered, an acquaintance brushed hurriedly past. She had dropped in for concert tickets, in response to a rambling phone call, and now could not leave quickly enough.

"She's really not well, is she?" the woman had said, with a pitying glance cast in my direction.

Upstairs, my mother came towards me on tiptoe, her body angled and her arms outstretched. A soft, grey fleece engulfed the top half of her, and her bare legs stuck out from underneath it like stalks. As she sank into my arms, she felt like a small bird plucked from its natural surroundings and flung into a wild and alien sky. Over her bony shoulder, odd piles of clothes and papers mingled with a disarray of books. Sticky notes, covered with garbled instructions, lay everywhere, and the furniture was pulled into a strange configuration like a child's fort. As I hugged her, my mother released a deluge of words in rushed and tangled speech.

That evening, my brother and his wife returned to their lives in London with some relief. Caroline had adjusted to my mother's strange behaviour, but Michael had shown a powerful urge to resist, as if he could bring Mum back to her senses through sheer force of will. During one long week, when she had stayed with them in London, she had overflowed the bath and shown a tendency to wander down the streets, pulling things distractedly from her bag and walking out of shops without paying. She could not even slow down enough to eat. In the midst of all the other chaos, she and my brother had argued. Once, to her enduring shame, she threw a glass of water in his direction, frustrated at his stubborn refusal to listen.

As their car pulled away, lights disappearing down the drive and away past the village green, the cottage had felt strange and lonely. The familiarity of home was tempered by the rabid scrabbling of my mother's mind as she fretted over lost papers, old arguments, and other detritus from an overstocked past.

Jet lag claimed the first night. I had locked up the cottage, returned the keys to their hook in the front hall, made sure my mother was safely in her room, and then retired to bed. Sleep mercifully shut everything else out. But at eight the next morning, I had been surprised by the sight of my mother's friend and neighbour at the foot of our steep stairs.

"I don't want to alarm you," she had said, with her classic northern understatement, "but I thought you should know that your mother has jumped out of the living room window in her nightdress. Take your time. Have a mug of something. She's over at Maggie's clutching a briefcase and drinking a cup of coffee."

In the living room, the window was still open. My mother had pulled a low table close to the wall for leverage, hoisted herself up, folded her rapidly thinning frame and squeezed through the window to drop onto grass several feel below. Later, with an odd mix of defiance and contrition, she would tell me that she executed a perfect skiing roll.

When I joined the party next door, Maggie was in her living room seated in an armchair near the wood-burning stove. Across from her, in a matching armchair, my mother perched, swathed in a long t-shirt and robe, slippers on, still clutching the brown leather briefcase to her chest. She was talking animatedly and waving the coffee cup in her free hand like a conductor's baton. Maggie, like any gracious hostess, was smiling sweetly and occasionally interjecting a word or two; she made no attempt to hurry her unusual guests.

When we eventually left, trooping home arm-in-arm, my mother had seemed curiously aware of her mania.

"I'm sorry I caused you such anxiety on your first night back," she said politely. "I don't know what got into me."

"Why did you feel you had to climb out of a window?" I asked.

"I thought you had all the keys," she confessed. "I found these papers I had been looking for, and I didn't want to lose them again. But I thought I was trapped inside."

Whatever it was that had got into her initially showed no signs of waning. At the height of the crisis, all three of her children came to be with her; my mother had galvanized us into a rare family reunion. For several days, we lived in the same house and worked as a close-knit team. While I offered emotional and practical support, Michael attended to my mother's financial concerns and Richard took her out for meals, often injecting his quirky humour to mitigate the gloom.

When we weren't helping Mum, we spent time looking at newspaper clippings of my father's squash and cricket matches, and we re-read the letters he had written to my mother during their courtship days. It was as if we felt he should be present during this crisis, or was already present as the great un-settler of my mother's mind.

On the last night before Richard returned home to Australia, he lay squeezed in my mother's spare bed with my father's letters strewn around him. As if he could order the past, and perhaps make sense of the present, he sorted the letters carefully by year and date.

I stayed on after my brothers left Lurgashall, acting as ballast so my mother could unravel knowing she would not get completely lost. While she sifted through old memories, pressing fears, and unexpressed regrets, I placed large stones in her hands for grounding and helped her take deep breaths. At times, I left the safety of my world and travelled into my mother's restless one where gremlins swept, cleared, and organised her mind. As dependence shifted its uneasy weight from one foot to the other, I learned to sway and lean with the currents of my mother's confusion, and my stay stretched from ten days to three weeks.

By the time I left, travelling to the airport with a hired driver and my mother in the back seat, she had begun to return to her old self; I was certain that she would fully recover. When we said goodbye, she clung to me, her ravaged body still strong enough to hold me fast. I wondered then if the seed of her complaint was our family's original fracturing. Perhaps, from the day of our father's death, my mother had held an impossible dream to mend what was broken and replace what was lost.

3

A CUP OF HAPPINESS

When I was born, my father famously declared: "My cup of happiness is full." Since he was not present at my birth, he made this pronouncement to Alice, the diminutive yet stocky housekeeper who was taking care of him. Perhaps she repeated the phrase later, or perhaps my father said it again when he arrived at the nursing home and held me in his arms; in any event, the story has become part of family lore.

I like to think that he said those words because he truly longed for a daughter and not because he felt competitive with his elder brother who had already helped produce a baby of each sex. All through childhood, Peter and Hubert had competed in friendly contests, imagining themselves on opposing professional teams in games of cricket, football, golf and squash. Since this habit of competition was ingrained, it is plausible that they also kept score of the number and type of their children. Yet if my mother is to be believed, the sentiment behind my father's declaration was real and the competition secondary. According to her, the phrase indicates a special bond: a proof of love between father and daughter set stalwartly against the disappointing fact of his death. It is difficult to reconcile these two things.

When my mother tells me the story this time, we are manoeuvring down a muddy path in a neighbour's field. In one hand, I am holding a small tape-recorder with which to capture my mother's words. The day is chilly for late-May, and we are bundled up in coats and scarves treading warily over the uneven ground. Around us, water has seeped into a marshland, and the trees, tipped with glistening spring, have lowered their heads in homage to the English rains. We cross the field and on a bridge that spans the lazy meanders of the river Lod, we pause.

My father's cup of happiness was rimmed with loss. The day before my birth, my grandfather's heart gave out, and he collapsed while chairing an annual meeting of the Football Association. He was just sixty-six years old.

Peter, devastated by the loss of his father, woke at 6 a.m. on the morning of June 8, 1963 sobbing uncontrollably. The intense emotion precipitated my mother's contractions, and they rushed her to the nursing home. That evening, while my father sat next to her reading the sporting results, the contractions began again. He left her to the messy business of birthing, and I came into the world just a few hours later, born on the heels of loss.

While my mother catches her breath, I wonder if my father's expression was a conventional phrase or something wrought from deep within him. And if his cup of happiness was full, did it mean he had nothing else to live for? Unanswered questions lie in his wake, left there like pieces of driftwood dragged up on the shore; their shape and texture awaken longing and a sharp stirring as lonely as a seagull's cry.

On the beaches of Crackington Haven, my parents collected sea trees - small burnished replicas of real trees worn smooth as bone. At some point in my childhood, I remember these trees glued to stones and left stranded, far from sea, on our bookshelves and tabletops.

"What was it like living with someone who had depression?".

My mother's face clouds over, and she tucks her head into the folds of her scarf, walking several paces before she answers.

"He would sit for ages with his head in his hands; he couldn't work. It was like a black curtain descending."

We trudge into the further field, our boots squelching through grass and puddles of water trapped in ruts and gullies.

"We just existed in a way. It was so hard for him. He was such a good person, such a fine man."

She does her best to conjure up a picture, offering examples of my father's thoughtfulness and his gentle nature. She tells me that he kept in touch with elderly people he knew as a boy, that he was always kind to his mother-in-law, and that he had decency and a sense of fair play in all of his sporting activities. But when she describes him as modest and retiring, she also hints that he was vulnerable to self-doubts.

Despite her efforts, my mother's words only drape my father's thin body; they do nothing to flesh him out. It will take continued investigation, and a sustained focus during this two-month visit, to give the story shape. As a family, we have tended to leave the dead buried, and I have lived off stray details, pecking at crumbs that seem to have no real relationship to the physical life my father had. It is hard to say exactly what I am looking for, and certainly other people's memories cannot substitute for my early loss, yet I am compelled to unearth the past and find traces of him. It is time now, while my mother is still alive, to confront the past and give voice to the stories; it is time to put flesh on absent bones.

Tucked in my wallet, there is a photograph of my parents; it is a black-and-white shot taken in a booth during their courtship days. In the photograph, their heads touch and they smile into the camera as the light goes off. My mother looks vibrant; her dark hair is swept off her face in a fashionable, wavy bob. Beside her, in jacket and tie, my father seems soft and effacing; his hair is parted on the side and smoothed across his head in a meticulous shine.

Theirs is a private world, a suspended state of happiness and promise out beyond a sea of family and rules. I have peered into this world, a shy voyeur, when I have read the letters my father wrote between 1949 when they met and 1952 when they were married. They are tender notes exposing the soft bud of my parents' love when nothing was more important than seeing each other and days apart felt like being becalmed.

I can picture him, a young man of twenty-two or three, seated in an armchair in the small living room of the London flat he shared with his sister, Pat. His slender body is hunched over a sheet of Basildon Bond writing paper, and his favourite pen is poised between finger and thumb. He has just returned from a weekend with his beloved. In his first sentence, he tells her he misses her already and then begins to describe the delicious breakfast he ate while travelling back on the train.

His letters are often like this – protestations of love interspersed with snapshots of recent or unfolding events, as if he cannot bear the thought of life passing without her. When he writes from a park, he describes being hit on the nose with a rubber ball; when pipes burst in the family home, the reader is right there in the flood and ensuing chaos. Everything that he writes about is a marker for the distance between them. Even his job at *The Cricketer* magazine is time stolen; he steals it back when he ignores the waiting proofs and piles of envelopes that need addressing. He tells her for the hundredth time how much she means to him, and waits impatiently for marriage when nothing and no one can separate them.

I have read these letters several times, recognizing the unbridled optimism and unchecked passion of first love. Won't it be dashed when he encounters my mother's human frailties and his own? How will the age difference play out? She is twenty-eight when this courtship takes place and he is twenty-three. And how will his depression affect their lives?

As my mother and I walk home along the single-track road, pressing our bodies into the hedgerow whenever a speeding car whips past, she talks obliquely of electrical shock treatments and hospitalizations that had no long-term impact; she tells me that my father's cycles of depression became worse and worse. Then she falls silent. This part of their history is vague and indeterminate. There is no chronology, no sense of the frequency or length of my father's visits to hospitals or private clinics. Instead, there is just the feeling that nothing really helped, and ultimately most institutions failed him.

My mother takes my arm, and we sway together like listing ships. The tape-recorder is turned off, and the only sound between us comes from our rubber boots hitting the tarmac in slow uneven beats. My father's demise has exaggerated our co-mingling and heightened the frequency of our sensitivity and need; if we were lost at sea, we would find each other trained to a signal of love.

She has lived alone now for twenty-six years. She laughs when she says that mothering is never over, yet I wonder how it is to have me back here delving in the past, asking questions about the grainy black-and-white photographs trapped in albums, and trying to form a narrative from the silences and buried history that make up our collective past. It is my father's story that I am unearthing, and yet his presence and absence feel inextricably tied to my own.

At home, my mother treads wearily up the stairs while I prepare tea: a delicate cup with lemon for her and a sturdy mug laced with milk and honey for me. As I search for biscuits, I hear her feet in socks rubbing across the carpet in the room overhead, and then the screech of her old filing cabinet makes the ceiling hum.

When she returns a short while later, she is holding something tightly between the fingers and thumb of one hand. It is a thin, green 1944 desk diary. My father's name is etched in ink at the top right hand corner, above an image of Alfred the Great, and inside, the pages are covered with his neat, boyish writing.

"Here, you better have this," she says, and I hold it cupped like the Holy Grail.

It is the second gift she has surprised me with. The first was a piece of cardboard on which my father had diligently copied thirteen words and their definitions - words like "palliate," "redolent" and, a particularly strange one, "gigolo" that he was apparently learning. Such precious traces are proof of my father's existence, signs that he did indeed walk the same earth. It seems that my questions have nudged loose small treasures from my mother's private store.

4

My father was born in London on December 3, 1927 at about the time that my mother first began school in Wales, walking several miles each way on her chubby six-year-old legs. Although he was christened Arthur Peter Doggart, as far as I can tell he was always known by his middle name. His father, Graham, was an accountant and an accomplished athlete well known in cricket and football circles. His mother, Grace, or Gramy as we called her, was among the first group of women to graduate from Cambridge, although evidence of this fact, in the form of a diploma, came years later when women were eventually accorded a more equal status in the world of men. After university, Gramy taught French for a while at a girls' boarding school, but her marriage to Graham in January 1924 turned her focus towards matriarchal and charitable duties. She was not a domestic woman - they had maids and cooks - but she had a strong sense of order and hierarchy; she liked things and people to be in their place.

My father's place was in the middle. His elder brother, Hubert, was an excellent sportsman and the proverbial apple of his mother's eye; his younger sister, Pat, also gifted athletically, held a lesser value in the household simply by virtue of being a girl. That left my father fatefully in-between. He had the same, if not greater, sporting potential as his brother, and certainly the same weight of expectation placed on boys, but he had an emotional disposition that would make it difficult to succeed on his mother's terms.

When the war began and my father was twelve, the family moved from London to a now-defunct house near Selsey on the Sussex coast. Brown House exists in my memory as an idyllic playground replete with tennis and squash court, an ancient cement swimming pool, a huge garden, and so many bedrooms that planning where we would sleep on summer visits kept us occupied on the car ride there. It was a generous place, perfect for entertaining friends, relatives, and the various colleagues associated with my grandfather's distinguished sporting life; it should have been a wonderful place for a child to grow up.

When I ask my mother what she knows about my father's childhood, she confesses ignorance but offers up two unconnected details: mandated hour-long rests after lunch and a special book where the children apparently signed toys in and out. This last detail, hotly denied by Peter's siblings, has calcified in my mother's memory from a conversation she had with my father years before.

"I would not have made that up," she assures me. "I distinctly remember the conversation taking place."

When I check this detail again with Hubert, he calls it "pure fiction." He also tells me that the hour-long rests were actually forty-five minutes and intended as a time for reading; he seems anxious for me to see the family in a rosier light. With a backdrop of photographs, group shots in studied poses where the family of five look robust and content, he speaks nostalgically of childhood and recalls the friendly games and competitions he shared with Peter. But when I ask Pat for her memories, she prefers not to speak about it; she tells me it was not a happy time.

In my father's old desk, the one that sits in the far corner of my mother's living room and is rarely used, there is a small red notebook filled with my grandmother's distinctly angular writing. It contains things she needed to remember - a recipe for her husband's "special cocktail," driving directions to Wembley Football Stadium, and notes about her favourite chocolates purchased on Old Bond Street from Charbonnel and Walker.

Most items in the book, pleasurable or practical, relate to measurement and order. Directions on where to find the fuse box and the main water taps in her London flat co-exist with the correct terms for hands at poker or quantities of champagne ranging from Magnum to Methuselah. And near the back of the book, a chart lists all the women in the family showing their size in nylons with a green cross next to anyone who would not wear tights.

Since Gramy was the only grandparent I knew, impressions of her remain seared in my memory with awed respect. Visits to her London flat evoked excitement tinged with anxiety, a state mirrored by my mother who would coax me into a dress and cue my behaviour all the way to Gramy's front door.

When she focused her energies on treats, like her wonderful Christmas parties, where she devised quizzes and chose interesting gifts for her extended family, Gramy brought people together. But this same will could just as easily annihilate anything messy or disappointing. One Christmas, for instance, when I had performed a playfully choreographed dance with my cousin, Evelyn, Gramy declared I was, "clumsy as an elephant" and urged my mother to enrol me in ballet.

My mother complied. Once a week for several years, I put on a pink tutu and performed my pliés and arabesques according to the whims of a Miss Faversham; she directed her girls in a voice like crushed glass, while her ancient mother pounded out tunes on a piano and vigorously marked time on her thigh. I never did become graceful in the way that my grandmother may have imagined. I liked the structured athleticism of the jumps, but loathed moving my body to an imaginary breeze or dancing as if I was a flower; my body was not set up for such public freedoms.

I felt a similar embarrassment when Gramy insisted on weighing and measuring each of her grandchildren on our annual visits. These fluctuating numbers were tabulated and carefully entered in her Visitors' Book, which lay out on her coffee table for all to see; unwittingly, she provided fodder for brotherly teasing which led to anxious mental comparisons about weight.

Yet despite this indignity, which my cousin Evelyn and I resisted in our early teens, visits to Gramy were a high treat. When my brothers stayed, along with their cousin, Simon, they went primarily to sporting events. When the girls stayed, we were treated to the theatre and, most spectacularly, the Pantomime. Sometimes, Gramy would order a limousine, and we would arrive at the theatre to emerge awkwardly under the gaze of an expectant crowd; occasionally, she would arrange for a performer at the Pantomime to single us out by name. She loved this kind of spectacle, and grand gestures were perhaps her way of showing love.

Still, beneath her confident exterior and her determined sense of what was right, my grandmother may also have been a nervous woman. When we would leave the theatre after a show, she would wrap our coats tightly around us and grip our hands painfully whenever we crossed a road. Now, I wonder if her careful choreography was insurance against the loss of another child. Back then, since she did not speak about my father, not even when I was old enough to understand, it did not occur to me to think of her as a mother who had lost a son.

A particular image of my grandmother lingers. Each morning of our stay, we were summoned to her bedroom where she received us, propped up on pillows and draped in a knitted bed jacket, with the remains of her breakfast pushed to one side. Peering at us periodically over the tops of her spectacles, she would read a list of the day's activities written on pieces of white card gripped between her arthritic fingers. Sitting upright next to my cousins, Evelyn and Victoria, in our semi-circle of chairs, I would listen for the jangle of Gramy's bracelet – the jostling of each of her grandchildren's names engraved on their ovals of gold. Arranged around her wrist and threaded together, this was a circle of family literally kept at arm's length.

It must have been hard when signs of my father's depression appeared during his teenage years; I imagine that the family did not know how to cope. There was relatively little information about depression back in the 1940s and 50s, and with English sensibilities being what they were, depression might have been seen as a self-indulgent weakness. But in whatever ways my grandmother responded to my father's fluctuating moods, she would certainly have believed that her actions were all for the best.

Photographs of my father as a pale and lanky teenager suggest vulnerabilities not evident before, and his eyes have a haunted look. But when I read his dairy, kept for one year when he was seventeen, there is nothing overtly disturbing in the pages. The diary has been in my possession for several days, but I have been reluctant to open it simply because anticipation is often sweeter than reward.

I take the diary down the lane to the millpond one morning, and read with my feet dangling over a low wall. The sky has lightened after hours of rain, and when the clouds disperse, the sun casts stray diamonds into the water. Occasionally, I am distracted by the passage of ducks.

My father is fascinated by war; I peer curiously over his shoulder as he re-lives school drills and studies newspaper accounts for details of allied advances, the number of planes shot down, and the frequency of bombs and gunfire. It is not what I expected, but I try to imagine life in 1944. Perhaps the war felt exciting to a young boy, as long as enemy planes passed overhead and no bombs dropped near their Sussex home. He may have felt part of something - a national identity that could bolster his fragile sense of belonging. Yet the diary also exposes the contrast between my mother's direct experience of war as a nurse and my father's youthful impressions. The realities of war could not have impinged greatly on a young boy who, in his leisure time, frequently had his hair trimmed, enjoyed eating out, and adored films – a boy who was not afraid to admit in writing that *Bambi* was "lovely."

While my mother dealt with bedpans, dressings, and patient care in the wards of St. George's Hospital in London, Peter, at seventeen, was still grappling with Shakespeare, Mathematics, French translation, Greek History and Latin. And while he could admire Churchill and celebrate the march to victory from a safe distance, he was not directly impacted in the way that my mother's family was. Less than a month after my father wrote his final entry in the diary, my mother's sister, Joyce, became a war-widow. Her husband's ship was torpedoed near Falmouth just three weeks before the end of the war. He died on the way to hospital leaving behind his pregnant wife, their two-year-old daughter, Ann, and their son, Jeremy, who was born several weeks later.

My father was an innocent; the simplicity of his life only accentuates the cruelty of his depression. I keep searching the diary for clues. He is punctilious about his designated chores, taking care of the chickens and collecting their eggs, but he seems to have had plenty of time to walk the family dog on the beach or play games with his sister, Pat. My mother has told me that the two of them would retreat to the relative seclusion of the viewing gallery above the squash court and play Monopoly for hours.

The only signs of tension in the diary relate to schoolwork. Some of the meticulous entries, squeezed into each day's one-by-four-inch space, refer to low placement in end-of-term exams. In one entry, my father admits that he has been kept back a remove. Were these small lines of worry precursors to larger cracks?

Any remaining space in the diary is filled with references to sport – games played at school as well as friendly yet competitive encounters with Hubert who often occupies my father's thoughts. Although he does not say this, I get the impression that Hubert represents a model to emulate. For while my father is relatively modest in mentioning his own achievements, he is acutely aware of his brother's success in sport, army training and military service.

Clouds are gathering and my body feels stiff. When I walk on past the millpond, my father's diary tucked under one arm, the resident male swan sidles towards me chest puffed, neck arched, hissing a fierce lament. Along the bank, piles of feathers excuse his truculence; he lets me pass then resumes punishing the grass with short, sharp thrusts of his beak.

The diary has revealed little, but depression did indeed seep into my father's life; he gradually lost ground. His housemaster at school suggested that he avoid exams; university became out of the question; he entered the Coldstream Guards, like his brother, but was invalided out after only a few weeks for mental health reasons.

When I picture my father, living in that large house by the sea, he is often dressed in jacket and tie conforming to a particular set of manners. He lives with an ear tuned to family discord and the constant fear that one of his dark moods may suddenly descend. He

28

wants to please his parents, and he wants to live up to his brother's example, but the dark moods make this difficult. He clings to the hope instilled by the good days and tries to imagine a fulfilling and successful life.

I turn right past the farmhouse and walk into the field, looking towards the tumbledown barn for signs of the owl that sometimes nests there. Ahead of me on the ground, delicate shells spaced at regular intervals look as if they have been deliberately placed there. But when I turn one over, the smooth mound on the top gives way to a jagged under-belly. It is the same with each one of the shells: not one egg has escaped the ruthlessness of whatever raided the nest.

THE SOUNDS OF SUMMER

"It's like living on the edge of a volcano," my mother declares, and in the same breath asserts that it is wonderful to have me home. On the eve of the Lurgashall Village Fête in early June, she is excited and garrulous. She is making cakes, unleashing a torrent of words in my direction and waving her spoons and spatulas as she mixes and beats.

With the warmer weather, my mother is increasingly hyperactive as if the light has sped up her germination. The behaviour mimics her previous illness, and I am wary and watchful as we clear the kitchen table of cake batter, parchment paper and tins. During the evening meal, we enact a parody of exaggerated slowness on my part and cartoon activity on hers. With measured words and slow speech, the child in me has abandoned my own ship and seeks control of the maverick craft. If I slow down enough, perhaps *she* will eat.

But my mother resists all attempts at control, and when the phone rings, creating a diversion, she shoots out of the back door as if expelled from a cannon.

"I'm just returning a brochure to friends," she trills, and disappears into the night. Soon, her voice rises above the hedges of a nearby garden where she is enjoying a glass of chilled wine.

By the time I have eaten and cleared up the kitchen, resentment, fed by worry, has burned a trail from my gut to my mouth. When the neighbour phones, and tells me with a laugh that they are sending my mother home, an irrational desire to punish her lies just under the

31

surface of my polite reply. And when my mother does return, flushed from wine and conversation, she is an easy target.

"I'm not your keeper, you know. You don't need to get someone who lives three houses away to phone and tell me you are coming home."

Her mood shifts like a swiftly moving river in the face of my anger. We retreat, treading warily on ground that is pitted with old emotional landmines. Anger hides my fear from view, but it comes forth later disguised as a thick, stifling blanket of remorse. It is the past creeping insistently into the present - my childish need for her to be well, accessible, and above all safe.

Several days later, after the frenzy of the fête has passed, we visit a farmhouse just across the green to see a squirming mass of eight-week old border terrier puppies.

"Isn't he lovely?" my mother murmurs, as she picks up the only puppy not yet sold and points out the white blaze on his chest.

"I'm not allowed to have one," she adds, dramatically, hugging the puppy close. "I can't bear it."

When I was ten, our golden Labrador had six female puppies. We kept them in a small room off the lounge using an old Wendy house as a barrier and covering the floor with newspaper and cardboard scraps. We named the puppies after various friends and charted their progress assiduously. Would Polly outgrow her weepy eyes? Did Rosie or Hattie have the biggest paws?

As they got older, the puppies spent their days in the back garden where I lay with them, lost in the milky smell of their breath, the pinch of their needle teeth, and the soft caress of their ears; puppy love was uncomplicated and pure. But eventually, they had to be sold, and with each one taken, my mother and I cried until we had returned to our usual two-dog state.

There are tears in my mother's eyes now, and she is clutching her treasure more tightly; it doesn't help that the dog's owner has said, with great compassion, that the puppy really suits her. *What puppy doesn't?* I think to myself, while raining down silent curses on the owner's amiable head.

While it is not strictly true that my mother cannot have a dog, her adoption of a golden retriever several years before offers a cautionary tale. Despite having had dogs for most of her life, Casper's food thieving, pillow chewing and general robustness had proved too much. His presence had helped trigger Mum's anxious condition, and we were forced, in the end, to find a more suitable home for him.

Although a terrier is a much smaller proposition, the puppy before us comes from a long line of wanderers; drastic action is clearly required. Ignoring the pleading looks of several women, I take the warm bundle from my mother's arms and manoeuvre her out of the cosy farmhouse to a chorus of puppy cries. In the car, she stares out of the window with her head turned away from me, nursing an aching heart. Mentioning the anticipated arrival of Little Bit later in the year does not help. I am met with childlike, unanswerable logic.

"But Little Bit is *your* dog, not mine."

We fall into silence for the next five minutes of our journey to Haslemere, one of several small towns conveniently located six miles away. Then, quite suddenly, my mother switches gear. Puppy temporarily forgotten, she begins to list various things that are worrying her: tasks to finish; where to park when we get to town; people she needs to contact; a thank-you she has forgotten; and concerns about her nephew, Jeremy, who has been staying with us for the past few days. Her speech has become hurried, and her shoulders are up around her ears.

"Slow down a little, Mum. Why not try some deep breathing?"

She shifts the tone of her voice, speaks more slowly and deliberately, but her mind is whirring like some haywire wind-up toy. I wonder if my cousin's visit has been too much. He is not well, and the medication used to treat his heart condition has had difficult side effects. He needs meals at specific times, and we have had to adjust our easy schedule for a more regimented one. He is also acutely aware of the processes of his body, giving us a running commentary on rushing blood, stomach pains, faintness and palpitations. My mother seems afraid that something might happen to Jeremy and we won't be able to cope.

"He is such a big man," she says. "What if he faints? How will we be able to get him up?"

At the supermarket, I am all efficiency, steering our course and driving our trolley as if we are taking part in a time trial. But when my mother suddenly wants to go to a fabric shop to buy pillows, and I cannot tell if this is a genuine need or a manic fancy. We go there, but I am monitoring her mood, and when she asks me to feel the density of various pillows, I give them no more than a cursory squeeze.

Back home, I cook and clean the kitchen as if my life depends on it, parrying my mother's sly jokes about searching the dustbins for discarded food and her references to my cracking the whip. I long to confide in Jeremy, but ill-health tempers his usual steady wisdom and limits his ability to focus on anyone else; when we speak of my mother, the conversation drifts quickly back to his own family concerns. He talks about his childhood, his father's death two weeks before he was born, and the anxiety he imagines that his mother, Joyce, may have passed to him in the womb. He also mentions his sister, Ann, commenting on her intelligence and the demands placed on her by family life: "She is a big engine," he says "in a small room."

When Jeremy's visit ends, my mother's false ebullience falters, and she seems frail. She is slipping between worlds, and her new blood-thinning medication makes her tired. Sometimes, she falls asleep in her garden chair in the middle of things. With tilted head, slack mouth, and soft rasping breath she once again resembles a small bird. When she wakes from these short forays into oblivion, she remarks guiltily that she "just dropped off" and then resumes her crossword or picks up the book she had been reading.

"Sometimes it feels as if I am waiting to die," she tells me one afternoon.

"What do you mean?" My voice raises an octave. "What is precious to you? What would you do if you only had a month to live?"

"I would spend the month worrying about whether I had done everything right," she replies. "I would wonder if I had left my affairs in order for you children, and if I had taken care of things."

"Mum, I am sure you have already done all that. What really matters to *you*? Are there things that you feel you have not done?"

34

She thinks for a moment, staring in the direction of the dilapidated bird feeder outside the kitchen window. She mentions being more skilful in music, talks of the singing she has given up, mourns the loss of foreign travel, and inevitably brings up the dog she tried, unsuccessfully, to adopt. I point out that these are all thing she can do something about – keep on with her music, sing, travel and even perhaps get a different dog that is more manageable. But she does not want solutions. She wants to express the ways in which her ageing body frustrates her and how it lets her down.

"You get to decide how that goes," I insist, making my needs more important than hers. "Are there things you want to do or places you want to visit?"

"Oh Julia, don't ask me such direct questions," she snaps. "I don't want to talk about it anymore. People should not have ideas above their station. I just need to be content with reality as it is."

The next morning, she hugs me. She has read the eight sheets of cardboard I had left on the kitchen table the night before listing thirty ways in which she has value.

"I should be turned in for crimes against motherhood," she confesses. "I feel ashamed for speaking that way; it's an insult to the gift of life. I will keep the notes as a salutary lesson."

We sit down to toast and marmalade, and I watch her across the table pouring her coffee out of the single glass cafetière. I know that I have shamed her, even if I did it in a loving way.

I wonder if she is afraid of dying. She has had recent health scares, sharp pains in her chest that will require an angiogram, and I have noticed a slowing down. She is still remarkable for her age, yet her body tires more easily and her aching knees make her walk with a shuffle and drag.

When I offer a form of energy healing, learned in America, she lies obediently on her bed with head tucked into a half-moon husk travelling pillow. Her eyes close and her aubergine cheeks soften; there is a blood blister on her lower lip, visible when she puffs out small pockets of air. As I cradle her head, bringing it gently in line with the rest of her body, the temples feel warm like risen dough.

I work my way down with a gentle "laying on" of hands; her

stomach and legs are cold, but the knees are fiery as if discharging the energy that propels her across tennis courts and up steep stairs. When I reach her feet, at the end of the session, her toes huddle, and two bubbles of skin protrude on the soles where she has met the earth again and again. My body feels still and calm. While she is sleeping, there is nothing to inhibit a complete offering of love; when she wakes, she seems refreshed and her eyes are clear like periwinkle or rain-washed forget-me-knots.

6

I wake each morning to the sounds of bird song and my head cushioned on two soft pillows under the sloping eaves in the spare bedroom – the room my mother has always insisted on calling mine. As summer begins to establish itself, the daylight creeps in with more demand. One morning, when the pink flowers on the apple tree are promiscuous from a night of rain, I leave the cottage quietly and turn left down the lane, walking between hedgerows humming in the morning sun. I am drawn, irresistibly, to the crumbling, snaking stonework of the Petworth estate.

As I follow the wall, its steady curving presence generous to ivy, my thoughts tend back to the image of my mother curled asleep on her bed. At night, the distance between life and death is paper-thin. My own and therefore *her* physical fragility assaults me with thumping blood and the sharp jut of hipbone. Sleep patterns are uncertain. If there are no jagged snores filtering through the walls, she might be reading with her legs propped on a stool or lying awake with eyes open. When death does pay a visit, I hope it will come as she wishes - gently in the middle of the night, or perhaps while she is resting in her beloved garden, or even in the act of raising her glass among friends.

The blue door surprises me - I must have passed it a hundred times - and it opens easily at my touch. Inside, the air is rich with a hint of wildness where nature has slipped out of her more formal wear. She beckons and I move forward, as if in slipper feet. In front of me, a small pond lies shrouded in mist, and beyond that, a path stretches off between trees while moss inches its way over roots.

Here in the south of England, beauty expresses herself quietly:

37

a yellow bird loops in and out of view; a rowing boat lies overturned and silent; cobwebs weave their fragile stories between the iris leaves. It is not my mother who fears dying; I am afraid of losing her.

Tomorrow, she will have her angiogram. Two weeks ago, when I took her to the hospital for her pre-angiogram tests, she had been unusually tired and out of sync. She had described herself as a disembodied spirit, someone without clarity or purpose.

"What *was* your purpose, Mum?" I had asked.

"Just existing, really," she had replied.

On my forty-fifth birthday, three days before the test, an assortment of my mother's friends had gathered under her apple tree. I had circled the chairs, American-style, and when the drinks were poured, small gifts given and received, and the cocktail sausages and quiches had done a couple of rounds, I had turned to the assembled company.

"Would you be willing to offer some piece of wisdom to the circle?" I had asked. "You know, something you have learned from your lives so far?"

There had been a startled silence. Hands holding glasses had stopped in mid-air, and a few people looked as if they would like to bolt.

"Are you confused about where you are?" one woman finally asked. "Do you realize you are in an English garden and not an American one?"

"If you want wisdom," someone else piped in, "you'll need to wait until the end of the evening when we've had more to drink. The English don't like to talk about themselves."

Amid the general laughter and the undercurrent of amused censure, my mother had stepped into the breach. She told a story about her eightieth birthday, when I had apparently "made" her read aloud favourite memories that people had written on little cards and placed in a "memory box" at my instigation.

"Julia is always asking horrible questions," she reassured everyone, and the conversation had drifted easily back to local gossip.

By the time I had returned with the next batch of finger-food, my outrageous request was more or less forgotten; it had been brushed aside as one of the lingering eccentricities of my American sojourn. If I wanted wisdom from these women who had lost husbands, raised children, survived illness, created businesses, weathered infidelities, and lived through huge generational change, then I would need to acquire it in more subtle ways. All they would offer as the evening progressed was their unanimous approval of the "stiff upper lip," and their credo of "getting on with life."

My mother displays a similar fortitude on the actual day of the angiogram. Having looked up the procedure on her computer, she is disturbed by the thought of a tiny probe making its way through wafer-thin arteries, but she does her best to hide any nerves. When the nurse arrives to set up the anaesthesia port, the two of them banter back and forth as if my mother is part of the team. And in fact, St. Richard's Hospital in Chichester *was* one of the places my mother used to work. It was also the place where she met my father in 1949.

I have heard the story of my parents' first meeting many times, yet it continues to delight me; it was so abrupt and decisive. My father had been at St. Richard's for a short while in a temporary porter's job, when my mother burst into the Almoner's office in her nurse's uniform. She demanded the key to the poison cupboard, flustering my father, and then exited as precipitously as she came. But she left a strong impression. Shortly after this, my father asked her on a first date to a football game.

It is a simple story, yet it contains so much – the hint of my mother's former impulsiveness and her ability to command a scene, as well as my father's innocence and his touching faith that the greatest treat he could offer her was a football game.

I wonder if she is remembering my father now, as we wait for the nurse to summon her and make light conversation about the paintings of sheep on the walls. How does one become an artist for hospitals we wonder? Is it the same as hotel art or does hospital art have its own unique form?

When the nurse finally wheels my mother away, it is after noon and time seems to be slumbering. The hours pass, as if each minute is stretching out its limbs. In the town, I visit bookshops and then retreat to a café, where I write in my journal and refuse to think about what the doctors might be doing.

By the time I return, the hospital halls are deserted and the reception bay is empty. The protocol for visits is unclear and signs on every door prohibit unauthorized entry; it takes a passing doctor to get me in to the recovery room. Once inside, I see beds loosely divided by curtains and two nurses doling out post-operative care. One of the nurses, a tall Scottish man, points out my mother lying on one of the beds receiving intravenous fluids. She smiles wanly and lifts a hand, assuring me that the procedure has gone well and she is fine.

When the doctor arrives, a slight Asian man with rounded corners and a sweet smile, he tells us that two of her arteries have heart disease, and that she is not a good candidate for surgery. He keeps apologizing for new hospital protocol that makes it impossible for him to wear a tie. My mother likes him; he is calm and sensible in his advice. Yes, a moderate diet is fine. No, she does not need to give up her whisky and ginger wine. Absolutely, she can still play tennis, but she needs to have an inhaler handy in case she feels constriction in her chest.

"If you use the inhaler three times at fifteen-minute intervals with no effect," he tells her cheerfully, "you should call an ambulance."

Far from being scared, my mother is galvanized by this medical prognosis. On the morning after the angiogram, she is up early. I hear her banging around in the kitchen and sorting things. She declares, while creating a substance to polish the pine furniture, that she is dispensing with her cleaning help and using the boost of my presence to shake herself out of old age.

"I was starting to decline before you came," she says. "I need to stay on top of things; none of this sitting around anymore. I think yoga might be good for me."

As the day wears on, she tackles weeds in her garden, checks on her allotment, takes care of washing and ironing, and then dives into her study for a prolonged session with bills. By early evening, she is exhausted.

"Do you think there might be some balance between all this activity and sitting around?" I venture.

40

She gives me a sceptical look. Over her shoulder, I notice the poster I made to commemorate her final downhill ski trip to Utah in 2005. She had been forced to miss two days of skiing due to an infection. One morning, we had left her in the rented house, surrounded by books and jigsaw puzzles, but returned to find the house empty - she had gone out snowshoeing.

"It was much harder than I imagined," she had confessed. "I kept falling down the wooded slope at the back of the house, and it was terribly hard to get up."

A few days after the angiogram, my mother calls me into the garden, excited by a new arrival. The pink clematis has a dark centre and its outer leaves are bruised pink. She has planted it against the fence that screens the compost area, and she invites me closer to see the delicate design woven around its heart.

As we walk around the garden, I notice other signs of recent activity: roses tied back, a noble hosta added to the line of impatiens in one of the flowerbeds, and lattice-work tucked behind a deep purple clematis that is covered in blooms.

"You must smell this, darling," my mother says, pointing to a fulsome rose, and I plunge my face into a nest of fragrant ruby petals.

It is hard and beautiful to watch her changing relationship to the things she loves. So much of her life has been defined by activity, and now she is learning when to resist old age and when she must surrender.

On the kitchen table, a gardening notebook lies open with a list of things needed in the allotment: lettuce seeds; purple sprouting broccoli; French bean plants; and some kind of cover to stop the birds from decimating the seedlings. We are late with our planting, and my mother has planned a trip to the local nursery to supplement our supplies; but by the time she has made soup, filling the kitchen with a heady aroma of garlic and mint, she is too tired.

As we eat, she periodically looks out of the window and names the birds on her feeder; then, she gestures towards a delicate bushy plant that has multiplied and poured a tumble of pink blossoms over one side of the garden shed.

"Just look at the beautiful escalonia," she says.

Later, when I pass the upstairs landing window, I catch a glimpse of her. She has pulled the wooden rocking chair into a comfortable position by the shed door and softened it with cushions. There she lies with her feet up on a plastic chair, eyes closed, cheeks puffing, catching the rays of a weak June sun. In front of her, a contraption of netting placed over her lettuce plants and secured with brooms looks like a pagan offering to invisible gods. Time slows imperceptibly; I feel the unconstrained immensity of our love as well as its particular human expression.

7

ABSENCE

When she is no longer here, my mother wants me to burn my father's letters. I wonder how it will feel to destroy these signs of him, these handwritten testaments to his presence here on earth. Almost sixty years after they were written, my mother is reluctant to read the letters herself; she finds it too distressing. Her love for my father is a vibrant, living thing.

Some years ago, my brother, Richard, cleaned out his London flat prior to emigrating. I was visiting when he brought down a bag of clothes intended for the charity shop. As we loaded the bag into my mother's car, she opened it, curious to see what her son was getting rid of and hopeful of finding small treasures like a sweater for the garden or a cap for tennis. Instead, she found a dark blue trench coat, old-fashioned and high quality, still in relatively good condition despite being more than three decades old. Instantly, she began to cry. It was my father's coat, one that he had worn regularly during their thirteen years of marriage.

It seems, in retrospect, almost as if my father's life came and went through the person of my mother – as if she could be life enough for the two of them. Certainly, my father's letters suggest that she is the one who made things bearable; she is the one who gave him hope. For amid my father's protestations of love, depression had cast a deep shadow.

"I don't really think there is much anyone can do," he writes. "I've just got to put up with it as best I can." And in another letter, he confesses, "It's jolly hard not to feel down with my trouble. It sort of gets right on top of one…how simply awful everything would be without you."

After my parents got engaged on April 7, 1951 the letters taper off to just a couple each month. Perhaps they were seeing more of each other then, or perhaps the engagement allayed my father's fears and he could relax. Their courtship had been intense. Now, he could focus on playing county squash and assessing promising new cricket players at various public schools, including the one that all three of his children would later attend.

My parents' marriage took place a year later on April 17, 1952. The couple look handsome on their wedding day; my father leans tenderly towards his bride, and she gazes at him with unabashed devotion. He was charming and sensitive - a man of unrealized potential who might thrive once he was free of family constraints. They are optimistic, naïve even, as they set up in their new London flat in Sheffield Terrace, heavily subsidised by his parents.

According to my mother, married life had little effect on my father's schedule. He continued working for *The Cricketer* magazine and the Squash Rackets Association - work that flowed naturally from his family connections and his sporting skills. He would sail off to an office during the week; at weekends, he enjoyed cricket and squash matches. My mother, on the other hand, was suddenly alone in a London flat without friends, without her job, and without the active life she had previously been living. She moved from room to room cleaning, planning meals, and looking forward to days when Peter had free time and they could play tennis or golf.

Within a few months, my mother slipped a disc in her back and was forced to lie still for three solid weeks. Since my father was working and she needed care, my mother stayed with his parents at Brown House. She likens it to being a patient in an isolation ward. She took all her meals alone and spent long quiet hours in a secluded part of the garden, while a kindly woman under my grandparents' employ took care of her basic needs. When she was back on her feet, my mother had to learn how to use all her muscles again; she had been re-born to an entirely different life.

In those days, it may have been commonplace for a wife to be absorbed into the traditions of her husband's family with little thought given to her habits and predilections. But nothing in my mother's relatively carefree upbringing would have prepared her for this. Although some areas of her life had been shaped by my grandparents' pastoral duties, my mother recalls an idyllic childhood playing on beaches, climbing rocks and exploring tide pools. She even found boarding school in East Sussex pleasurable, despite being miles from her home in Wales, and her natural inclination seems to have been towards a robust and expressive enjoyment of life.

In her new role as wife, however, my mother had to navigate temperaments she did not necessarily understand. Her in-laws would visit every six months by appointment, and visits back to them, also by appointment, were sometimes marred by stress and simmering resentment when my mother perceived insensitive treatment of her beloved Peter.

"I cried when we spent our first married Christmas with them," she confesses. "We had it in a hotel instead of a home."

I picture my mother in this formal environment, anxiously monitoring my father's moods and doing her best not to upset things. Her instinct would have been to protect my father and shield him from anything difficult or unpleasant, but the tensions would have been alien to her. And although she came to greatly admire and appreciate her mother-in-law, the distance between them in those early days must have seemed immense.

Perhaps it was like learning a new language; no matter how much she studied and practiced, my mother would never become comfortably fluent and thus would always feel at a slight disadvantage. And since they were reliant on my father's parents for financial help, they might have remained somewhat under the family shadow. It would have been important, in such circumstances, to feel that they could create distinct lives of their own.

When I ask my mother about their decision to have children, we are seated at her kitchen table with the tape-recorder between us. As she opens up memories and they slip through her net, raw and tender, she hauls back the ones that seem too private, too exposing.

"We weren't going to have children at first," she says. "We were afraid it would put too much of a strain on your father. I sometimes wonder if we hadn't had children.... " She trails off, leaving the rest of her sentence clear but unspoken.

On the ledge of the kitchen window, a basil plant is struggling to survive; it needs water. While I take it over to the sink and let the tap run, my mother continues her story. She describes the hopeful beginnings of family life, almost as if the story is still unfolding, and emotions play across her face like seasons.

When my mother became pregnant with Michael, three years into their married life, my parents moved out of London and into a small house in Leatherhead, Surrey. The anticipation of a child would have amplified feelings of love and independence and also affirmed the maturity and focus of their marriage. It must have been a momentous time. With Michael's birth in September 1955, followed by the acquisition of a Golden Retriever puppy called Ben, and then a second move to a larger house with a bigger garden, everything seemed in place.

Two years after Michael's birth, the new family enjoy their first holiday together. In a perfect tableau, they appear in three side-by-side photographs in one of the Brown House Visitors' Books. The photograph in the middle shows Michael on the beach with bucket and spade; the ones that flank it are a matched pair, with my father carrying Michael piggyback-style in one photo, and my mother duplicating the pose in the other. They are smiling, wind-tousled and relaxed. For the next several years, they would appear each summer as a happy family, gratefully enjoying the hospitality at Brown House.

Life had a whole new focus; the only question was how my father's health would hold up under the pressure of these new family demands. For despite appearances, things at home were not always easy, especially when my father had a deadline at *The Cricketer* magazine.

"I was always pulled between taking care of Michael and helping Peter," my mother tells me. "He sometimes struggled with the articles he had to write, and he would make me listen to them,

46

asking me over and over again if they sounded all right."

She talks on about Michael and how it must have been hard growing up with a father who was present and playful one day and then inexplicably withdrawn the next. On good days, father and son would play football or cricket together. Michael still remembers hitting a shot over the neighbours' fence and running for 230 while Peter looked for the ball. He has also told me that he enjoyed football so much he would hold on and wet his pants rather than go indoors. But on bad days, his father would have been short-tempered or unable to play with him at all, and Michael would have had to entertain himself.

"Our life was quite insular; we muddled along with very little outside contact," my mother explains. "Hardly anyone came to visit us, and we didn't go out and socialise. Peter was even afraid to go on dog walks at times; he thought people would wonder why he wasn't at work."

It is difficult to imagine my mother in such socially parched circumstances. Behind her now, on a set of small white shelves, are rows of cookery books bulging with additional recipes that she uses to entertain her friends. Whenever she is feeling low, she hosts a tea party or has people round for drinks accompanied by her homemade cheese biscuits. She must have felt quite lonely back then and continually anxious about my father and about interactions between father and son; the family's happiness and equilibrium, it seemed, was always tied to my father's mental state.

"He was so afraid of you being ashamed of him," my mother continues. "And yet having children gave him so much pleasure."

In the year that my father left us, Michael sent two successive letters from his boarding school in which he asked about my father's rank in the army. It was the kind of thing a boy might ask if he wanted to boast to friends, but the questions must have sent my father into paroxysms of self-doubt. How could he tell his son that he was not like other fathers? How could he say that he had been invalided out of the Coldstream Guards? How could he explain that depression had robbed him of a full life?

Among the collection of old family slides that I have scanned during this visit home, my favourites ones show father and son working together in the garden. They tie up bean plants, mow the lawn with appropriately sized machines, and take tea breaks on the back patio where they drink out of fat-lipped green china mugs. Between them, the family dog looks like a sheaf of burnished corn, and the scene appears tranquil and safe. What if things had stayed that way? What if Michael had been the only child?

My mother had several miscarriages before Richard arrived, round faced and ruddy, in June 1961. In a group photograph, taken at Brown House on the occasion of Richard's first visit, my father appears slight and even under-nourished next to his taller, broader brother. Although his handwritten entry in the Visitors' Book describes an enjoyable shared holiday, the anxious facial expression is back.

My arrival two years later, prompting the line about my father's cup of happiness, must have been the final wished-for straw. Three children were a gift *and* a burden, pulling my mother's attention away from our father and diminishing his life at the same time that it gave him pleasure. He had helped to create three beautiful lives, but my father had edged himself out of the picture.

8

When my father left us, his absence became a presence; the loss of him made the world tip and tilt, as if the legs of our furniture had been unevenly sawn off. Our father had died of pneumonia – a technical truth – but Richard, who was nearly four, did not believe it. He banged his head against the wall and demanded to know when his father was coming back. I was not yet two. Whatever I felt had no verbal expression; I lay in my mother's arms, and her sorrow seeped through my skin since it was fresh and permeable. It was Michael, old enough to really know my father, who was told the truth.

Imagine a small boy in grey flannel uniform shorts and a thick shirt. His knees stick out below the flannel, and his hair is slicked over to one side of his moon face. His eyes seem wistful, like his father's, and his ears have a tendency to stick out. He is nine years old when he is called to the Headmaster's office at his preparatory boarding school. He arrives to find his uncle there, but he looks past him towards the gym shoe cupboard, wondering what he has done wrong and what punishment will be meted out. But instead of physical punishment, he hears that his father is dead.

All afternoon, the small boy runs up and down the grassy wing of the football field, repeating the words, "Daddy is dead, Daddy is dead." He wonders why he can't cry then, or later when he is teased about it. In the "grin and bear it" world of English boarding school, he soldiers on. His letters home carefully include his siblings, but he makes no mention of "Daddy" at all.

It is strange now to realize how rarely we spoke of my father. The shock of his death made us mute, and my mother's sadness seemed to surround his memory like an impenetrable wall. It was the silence, even more than the death, which seemed to shape our lives, as if our father had not existed at all.

Yet his death marked us. We became a close-knit clan who protected one another from the clumsy silence of relatives and the probing words of strangers. The stem of our family had split, and we alone reserved the right to hurt and punish each other for things we could not control. Michael, with distinct memories of a father, and an understanding of what he had lost, grew one way; Richard and I, with an emotional but not cognitive sense of loss, grew in another. My mother, meanwhile, held the uneven weight of it all; she tucked away her grief.

If my father's shadowy presence was insubstantial, my mother's robust figure almost made up for his loss. Perhaps she used the skills she learned as a nurse during the war, when she lived in Spartan quarters in Knightsbridge with no glass in the windows, cold baths, and only a gas fire for heat; she did her job then with guns going off, plaster falling in the operating room, and the tense eerie silences prior to a direct bomb hit. Some part of her may have been prepared for this devastation; as a child, I counted on this.

Each act of love offered by my mother - reading with me by the fire, telling me made-up stories, slipping a hot water bottle into my bed – was proof that she would never leave us. It was her love, ragged sometimes yet always dependable, that knit our small family into a workable shape.

We survived, thrived even, with my mother at the helm. Michael was her able lieutenant marshalling us for games and household duties. He drew up a chart once to assign us different cleaning jobs and then happily monitored our progress from his perch on the flat-topped dishwasher we affectionately named Gladys. He also invented nicknames – one hundred and fifty nicknames for Richard and a more modest number for me, modelled, for no apparent reason, after a horse trainer called Ryan Price.

These are affectionate memories, and yet, when I look back, childhood seems remote - an innocence floating just out of reach, as if someone had placed a transparent barrier between my early life and me. When Michael reads a draft of my manuscript, he asks why he and Richard are such one-dimensional figures. His question makes me dredge the past, trawling for memories that may have sunk below the surface or snagged on weeds. I pull up instances of mock wrestling matches, when Richard and I would pin Michael to the floor and he would beg for mercy, as well as elaborate games acting out ludicrous stereotypes of the American West. Once, in the midst of battle, Richard threw a spear at a young boy called Gary and pierced his thigh; the injury required numerous stitches.

During the holidays, when my brothers returned from boarding school and we were all together, Michael enrolled us in Olympic-style games on the long lawn at the back of the house. When we weren't playing cricket or football, we were running interval sprints and leaping over tray tables and other props that he had carefully arranged. He would record our times with a stopwatch and solemnly write them down. Later, when I developed a passion for tennis, Michael enthusiastically supported my training regime, even when I missed family holidays. He would urge me to toughen up mentally so I could win more games; he seemed eager for my success.

Yet despite these memories, there is no coherent story line with my brothers, just short sharp instances as they came and went. Perhaps our father's death disturbed the link between us, or perhaps it was a simple case of logistics that made our connection more remote. When my brothers were away at school, accessible only at weekends, my mother would take me to watch them play sports. These were long days, usually begun in a panic because my mother was late and consisted of hours on the sidelines rewarded, eventually, with tea and cake. When we drove home in the evenings, I would invariably fall asleep in the car and my mother would have to carry me to bed.

At home, my mother remembers me as a happy little girl, and most of the time it was true. At my small local day school, I was praised for having a "friendly and affectionate manner without any tiresome moods," and in the classroom, I was "never silly or uncontrolled." If I was boisterous in the playground - frequently falling, playing football with the boys, and using the monkey bar frame until blisters covered my hands – I was also easy to keep in check. When I hit a small boy in the face with a football one afternoon, making him cry, I was summarily banished from the small boys' game.

I glean these snippets from my early school reports - documents that support obedience and conformity. One official report card reads: "Writing has been very strange at times, changing its slope and its size. Julia must make up her mind to keep to one style and not mix them all together." When I fail to conform, there is a cutting follow-up: "The 'new styles' are seldom as good as the original, and Julia's writing has varied from good to rather peculiar."

A more revealing comment is tucked into my autumn report for 1970: "Julia finds it difficult to learn something new calmly, and blind panic hits if she cannot immediately understand what is required of her." This comment suggests there may have been subtle strands of anxiety under the solid earth of home.

On a holiday in Cornwall with my mother and Richard when I was nine, I hoarded paper napkins on the top shelf in the tiny bedroom closet. My mother remembers this as a charming incident demonstrating the quirkiness of my character, but I am not so sure. I had other techniques for maintaining order. If I wiggled one toe, then I had to wiggle the same toe on the other foot; if one finger moved a certain number of times, then the duplicate finger must do the same. In this way, I staved off small irregularities such as my mother bent anxiously over the household accounts or my brothers aiming their youthful curiosity at my female body.

When I was eight, life was measurably good. I started a new school with a wonderful Scottish headmistress who propelled her imposing figure along the corridors with a pug dog named Roly in hot pursuit. Together, they ruled strictly but with wisdom and benevolence. It was Miss Cameron who had designed the uniform I loved of kilts, white shirts, and patterned Fair Isle sweaters. I even had a sporran - a leather pouch attached to a belt that hung in front of the kilt – where I kept money for sweets.

Each weekday, I rode the train and then walked to school with my best friend, Alison. On days when my mother worked as a secretary in London, Alison's house became my second home. Her mother, Rosemary, taught us how to cook. She began with the correct method for hand washing and worked up to things like cheesy potatoes and meringues. We wrote all the recipes down in a little red book. While our house was often jumbled and chaotic, and my mother almost always late for things, Alison's house, with mother and father intact, was reassuringly ordered and predictable. Despite this, I was always glad to return to the comfort and disarray of home.

Once, I chased Alison's brother, Anthony, around their back garden and accidentally stepped on his precious kite. He howled over the mangled remains, and I was so terrified that I ran away. I walked several miles home only to be confronted by an empty house. Fortunately, a neighbour found me and brought me back. When Rosemary saw that I was safe, she was flooded with anxious relief and exorcised this feeling by turning me over her knee and spanking hard. But when my mother arrived, she did not even scold; she understood the depth of my suffering, and she drew me into her arms for a long hug.

It is physical memories such as these that linger, mute and expressive at the same time: the firmness of my mother's arms; the sting of a football catching me at the back door; the needle teeth of puppies; my hand forcibly caught between trousers and soft, yielding flesh. When snow fell one year and turned to ice, I rode my toboggan into a signpost and jarred my hips so badly that Alison's father had to carry me home. Another year, my bicycle hit the side of a car, and there are photographs of me sitting on the garden bench with one arm held in plaster.

These are hard physical events that remain in my body like small deposits from the past, stacked there in layers and pressing on my bones and joints. But there are no such memories of my father; there are no physical links to him.

"You would have missed him terribly," my cousin Ann tells me, "because you were always with him. Your father carried you around on his shoulders all the time."

No physical sensations accompany these words. I wish I could reach back and feel the tweed material of my father's jacket. I wish I could nestle into his neck, play with his thinning hair, or cup my hands around his anxious face. If I had known then that moments with him would be so rare, I would have soaked them in, printing them indelibly in my consciousness, so that I could return there again and again.

It just isn't the same when others say, "Oh, your father loved to carry you around," or, "He was so happy to have a little girl." These are words riding in a clear blue sky like distant wings. I cannot taste, touch, smell or feel him. There is an absence at the heart of things.

9

EXILE

I am twelve years old, and my mother is driving me to boarding school about two hours away. My new school uniform and all the other trappings of a full-time boarder are tucked in a trunk in the back of our car. The drive seems desolate, and the road rolls endlessly across the cold English countryside where everything is exposed.

The school itself sits high on a hill, and a chill wind whips the trees that stand sentinel as we approach the flat, symmetrical building. All along its bland face evenly spaced windows give nothing away, and playing fields stretch out in uniform green as if they were rolled out freshly each day.

We park and carry my things into the boarding house. It is a long two-story building connected to the main school via a passage punctuated by identical arches; there is a minimal separation between school and after-school. Upstairs, tiny cubicles replicate each other as if there has been a breeding frenzy, and there is nothing to distinguish each bed, basin, wardrobe, table, or chair. Three-quarter walls and a thin curtain mark off our small territories, and the sounds of girls settling in rise and fall around me as stray billows of sound.

When we finally hug goodbye, my mother and I hold on tightly; we say reassuring things about half-term and weekend visits, and then she drives away. I watch her move slowly over the disapproving speed bumps and past the same line of trees, until she eases out onto the main road and is swallowed from view. A vast emptiness surrounds me.

❧

In my mother's ugly grey filing cabinet with the broken handle, there are plastic bags full of envelopes: a bag for each of her children's boarding school letters. At least one letter in each collection contains a desperate plea for release. Richard's first letter home at age seven, for instance, is a compelling masterpiece with inventive spelling: "Deary Mummy," he writes. "I dt't like the food they give you. I hate the school and its horrid. I want to come home." But by his third letter, he seems to have adapted; he is sharing news and requesting that my mother send tins of "spigety."

My first letter, written on purple paper with a crinkly edge, recounts a disturbing incident in which my housemistress poured someone's mug of hot chocolate over the floor, smashed the mug, and then made the girl clean it up; I refer to this event as a "great saga" without seeming shocked. The four letters that chase this one are newsy and focused on visits home. It is the sixth letter, written exactly two months and six days into my first term, that contains my plea for release: "Dear Mum," I write. "It's horrible here. I'm miserable."

What follows is a strong argument for the benefits of day school and the importance of having time for my tennis. I promise to work hard and make Mum proud of me. I pledge to help with washing up, cooking, dog walks and other household chores if only she will let me come home: "I hate it here; I must leave, I really must."

Sitting in my mother's cottage, reading these letters from a distance of thirty-four years, I cannot get to the truth of them. I do not know exactly why I asked to come home or why I chose to stay. It may have been that the alternative path of day school was ultimately not that appealing; my brothers were away at school and university, and my relationship with Mum had entered those challenging teenage years.

Whatever the reason, I stayed at the school for four years and ameliorated the horrors with a stint of weekly boarding. For about a year, my mother and I endured agonizing journeys. Sundays were the worst. As we drove back to the school, I would blast music and sob out of the car window most of the way there. My mother would deposit me, miserable yet resigned, and then, armed with a thermos of strong black coffee, she would make the long drive home in the dark struggling to stay awake.

"It can't have been all bad," my uncle expostulates, when he reads my description of school. "What about teachers who inspired you?" His own years as a history teacher in public school, and then as a headmaster, have no doubt influenced this question. But a quick survey in my mind produces no outstanding memories of academic classes, just random scenes. My French teacher, for instance, wore a wig, and we made fun of her when it sat unevenly on her head or when she took long minutes to write on the board, tracing a line in the dust with the tip of her little finger; now, I realize she had probably suffered a stroke or perhaps lost her hair to cancer. I also remember my Latin teacher; she used to complain that I grinned too much and urged me not to rest on my laurels. And my sewing teacher accused me once of hiding my work, when in fact it was just misplaced.

Boarding school had been a rude awakening, a place where institutional conformity and coldness replaced the care and dependency that had grown in the wake of my father's death. At boarding school, vulnerabilities were a weakness and spontaneity was crushed before it could breathe. The emphasis was all on surface behaviour, and at the end of each term, a long list in the main changing area showed a public tally of the number of points each of us had been awarded for our tidiness and posture.

It was not my intention to be difficult, but I was seen as either too diffident or too brash. I did well in expressive subjects like English, Speech and Drama, Art, and Music, but my deficiencies in Maths and Science were now given additional weight. I felt as if I was unseen and misplaced. I wrote home during classes with damning asides about my teachers. In one letter, an elaborate chart shows the remaining thirty-seven days of one term divided into subjects and rated with classifications like "ugh" or "good." The headmistress began penning ominous warnings at the bottom of my reports: "I hope Julia will act on advice and get herself organized before it is too late."

Perhaps boarding school simply exposed the cracks in our

family configuration, and revealed the gaps left when my mother was not there to act as a lynch pin. Or perhaps it was the school that was exposed - its mindless discipline and academic demands unable to cover its deficiencies of care. It was a wretched place for puberty and an even worse one to discover an attraction to girls. Close friendships, especially with older girls, were frowned on and nervously extinguished. My early crushes and adolescent longings were deemed inappropriate, and admiring notes passed during class were intercepted and banned.

My happiest times were playing lacrosse or tennis; I was good at these sports and earned easy recognition. But then my body betrayed me. My breasts grew out of proportion to my athletic frame, and I felt slow and clumsy. Swimming class was a nightmare, and I sometimes wore two swimsuits in a misguided attempt to appear smaller. When my period came, my mother called it "the curse" and advised wearing a thick pad attached with safety pins that showed in gym class through our hideous brown knickers. It had been an important lesson learned: mothers do not always protect you from things that hurt.

Mid-way through my boarding school experience, there is a definite shift in the tone of my letters home. Suddenly, they are more veiled and deliberate. Gone is the childhood prattle that had danced in the lines; in its place, a more stoical, solicitous tone indicates a new sense of responsibility that seems directed towards my mother. Instead of expressing *my* feelings, I reassure *her* in gentle yet anxious tones, as if I am afraid she will break or unravel.

This noticeable shift comes shortly after my mother pulls me out of school for a special conversation in which she sets the record straight about my father; she corrects a lie, and, in doing so, she ploughs up the smoothed-out terrain of my early childhood. What had seemed solid now cannot be relied on at all.

"Your brother is getting teased at school. That's why I pulled you out. There is something I need to tell you. Something I have to say."

I flash back to another day, also in the back of the car with my body pressed against the seat in tense fury, tears flying out of my eyes like small time-bombs and my head resolutely turned to the side. On that day, the sounds coming from my mother's mouth had been like wisps of straw tossed in front of an oncoming flood. We had just come from a small antiseptic office, where I had held my dog's paw while the vet in the white coat administered the injection that made him dead. I had stroked the wire-haired head and tough little body with paws that dug, and I had hated my mother. I had hated her because she could do nothing and because she was seeing me laid bare, flesh exposed, mourning this terrible loss.

"It's about your father. About the way he died."

We buried the small body in the earth of our garden, among flowers that Johnny would have rooted up in spring. He was a proud dog, trotting through his territory like a very small king. He was a terrier, known for his ferocity yet ready to lay his head on your resting feet or jump into your lap and make a temporary home.

"I thought Dad died of pneumonia. That's what you said."

Johnny died because he had one fight too many – a tussle with a fox down a rabbit hole or another dog eying him the wrong way. The wounds were in the right mid-section of his body, and they just wouldn't heal. Cancer, the vet said, with tumours inside.

"I told you and Richard it was pneumonia, because I didn't know what else to say. I didn't want to upset you. And it was true. He did have pneumonia when they found him; he never regained consciousness before he died."

One time, Johnny was found at a neighbours' house chasing the bitch in season around the kitchen table. The owners were furious, and we had to go and retrieve him. But for Johnny, it was just another day.

"You have to understand. It was so difficult back then. Your grandmother was telling me what I should do. That's why none of you ever came to the funeral; I would do it all so differently now."

Funerals and birthdays need to be marked. One birthday, Michael carefully pulled all the rinds from his serving of streaky bacon and made a special nest of them in Johnny's dog bowl. We pulled a chair in close, hoisted him up, and Johnny ate those bacon rinds right out of his dish with paws on our grey-checked kitchen table.

"I remember so clearly the day it happened. Your father and I had been decorating the house. I thought things were good; he was upbeat. He told me he was going to the shops to get some things. Should I have known? He didn't let me talk about his depression when things were good; he thought it would jinx him. He was gone a long time. I began to worry. I called Mrs. Skinner to come and watch you, and I went out to find him. No sign. I got the call later that evening. I rushed to the hospital, but he never regained consciousness; he never even knew I was there."

What kind of consciousness does a dog have? Did he know when we took him to the vet's that it was for the last time? How did it feel to drift off to sleep, to watch the shapes in the room grow dim, and to feel the slab of the hard table under his body and my hand gently touching him?

"Your father took an overdose. They found him near where we used to walk the dogs sometimes at the edge of the world. You know, near the concrete bunkers and the parking place covered in leaves. He had a photograph of the three of you, a Bible, and a handwritten note."

A body gets hard and then it doesn't feel like the dog you once knew. Johnny went from being warm and alive to something so still that my tears were the only things moving in the room. And then the vet gently picked him up and took him away. Death is a hard fact that renders you powerless. There is a burning. The body is gone. A life is eradicated in moments.

"Do you have the note? What did he say?"

"I didn't keep it. I don't know why. He loved you so much. It must have been a hard decision for him to leave you. We have to honour his decision; we have to honour him. It's not something we will talk about outside the family; he wouldn't want that. He was an intensely private man."

How private is it to say goodbye to your dog in the presence of someone you don't know?

"Why didn't you tell me? Why didn't you tell me? Why did he leave me that way?

10

If you break a small milk bottle, the kind you used to get in school back in the eighties, the glass shards are really good cutting tools. The best place is the knuckles. You can gently cut the skin, and each time you bend your fingers the cuts open and bleed a little. It is a sharp stinging sensation. The pain does not last long; it is just enough to make you feel alive.

It is good to do this over a basin in the downstairs cloakroom at school so that you do not make a mess. No one notices if you keep your sleeves pulled down. If they do notice, it is easy to say that you scratched yourself on a rosebush or you fell over and grazed your knuckles.

Some days, this may not be enough. It may feel like dull routine, and there are already so many routines here. The weekends are the worst. Most people have gone home, and there is nothing much to do. It feels good to turn music by The Stranglers up loud and open the windows so the sound rolls out over those indifferent, manicured lawns. There are several angry phrases in one of the songs that are worth repeating. Perhaps the words will disturb the smooth surface of the school with its bland façade and row upon row of unblinking windows; but no one even makes you turn it down.

Alcohol takes the edge off things, but then you feel numb again. One evening, you celebrate a friend's birthday by sneaking out and joining her on a drinking binge. This includes a bottle of sherry and neat Bacardi Rum, bought quite easily from an Off License back then. But sherry and rum are not a good mix. When you sneak back to school by way of the lacrosse fields, the green horizon slants and tilts, and it is difficult to stay upright.

One of the back doors is open, thank goodness, and you clamber up the stairs to the attics and then cross over to your side of the building. When you fall down the stairs on the other side, because you are limp and legless, you feel nothing; then, you climb into bed fully clothed. You are sick in the night, but you don't remember waking up; perhaps you are lucky to be alive. When you are sent to the headmistress, she berates you but she does not really care. You are leaving the school soon and will become someone else's problem; you have no real value to her.

When you play with a razor, it looks neat and efficient. You are actually a little nervous. You know perfectly well that you have no intention of truly harming yourself. You just feel angry and let down. You do not like being lied to. Someone has changed the whole look and feel of your world.

You press the blade against the skin of your hand, just below the right thumb, and pull back quickly without looking. The skin splits easily like a ripe nectarine. Suddenly, you are afraid. It is your right hand, a hand that needs to be flexible and free. You tape the cut tightly with plaster so it won't open during lacrosse practice the next morning, and you reassure yourself that it will heal. You even tell a friend what you did, and when she chastises you, it is clear that you are loved.

What is the gift in the lie, you wonder? From now on, you will look even more intently below the surface of things. You will be alert to the unspoken, the hidden, and the unknown. You will sense when people are telling the truth and when they are not. You will probe, question, and uncover until you understand. Assuming that there is always more to a situation than is apparent, you will be slow to trust and furious if you are betrayed. Your mind will make up for any deficiencies in your emotional landscape as you edge intimacy aside and keep people at a distance.

For you are not like the others, and nothing can make you like them. You have a father who killed himself. You have a father who found the world so unbearable, even though you were in it, that he took his own life.

11

HEADLINES AND LINEAGES

"An old woman was stabbed in Epsom."

My mother likes to read me headlines as soon I come downstairs in the morning for tea and toast.

"Do you mind not reading that to me first thing in the morning?"

"These are facts you need to know."

"Mum, there are a million facts in the world, why this one?"

When I return later for a second cup of tea, and one more slice of my mother's homemade bread, toasted and covered with marmalade, she has a new headline.

"There's a crisis in Burma. All of the officials seem to be corrupt."

"Mum, I really don't want to hear that."

"But this is going on in the world, you need to know."

"Well, at least I can choose *when* in the day I hear about it, and I don't want to hear it as soon as I wake up."

In fact, I am resistant to bad news and resistant to second-hand grief that does not know the true circumstances of its grieving. Bad news stirs my mother's anxiety. Her face creases like paper; her tone lowers like a hushed and breathless wind. And although we busy ourselves during the day, anxiety will follow us like a restless dog.

In the pub that evening, a refuge when neither of us feels like cooking, our conversation seems fated. I am now midway through my visit home, and we have passed the stage of making polite conversation. My mother searches for something to say.

On the table between us, a tiny crystal candleholder catches the movement of the flame and sends it dancing across the wood in a play of light and shadow; with her hands caught in this dappled expression, my mother starts a much-rehearsed story about a woman in the village who is guilty of social climbing. My hackles rise. Telling stories in a way that overtly diminishes people, or purports to define them, touches a raw spot.

"I wouldn't want to be held to past actions like that," I tell her, keeping my eyes fixed on the flickering light patterns.

My mother moves back in her chair and raises her hands, as if disowning her own words, and the story dies in the air. But each telling deepens the groove.

It reminds me of another story my mother likes to tell. Some years after I left the all-girls boarding school, a parent of a friend took it upon himself to tell my mother that I used to cut my hands. Through his carelessness, or intentional malice, he distorted the truth and planted a small seed of horror in my mother's fallible heart; it took root like the twisted offshoot of a banyan tree, and she nurtured it. But the facts of her story are all wrong.

Without consulting me, my mother obsessed and imagined until the picture that she created bore no resemblance to the truth. The relatively harmless pastime of superficially cutting the backs of my hands became muddled in my mother's mind with an entirely different event.

I was ten or eleven, and Michael had sent me out onto the balcony that led off two of our four bedrooms at home.

"Go get my slippers," he had told me. "I left them outside, and I need them back."

It was night; the balcony was cold and dark, and the slippers were nowhere in sight. I had hurried back to the window, but it was locked tight. I knocked, called out, pleaded with Michael to let me back inside where it was warm and light. And then I banged on the window, harder and harder, until my right hand smashed through the glass.

My mother took me to Epsom Hospital, accompanied by Mrs. Skinner who helped my mother in the house and was relied upon for all states of emergency. I still remember her kindly face hovering above me during the car ride, as she fed me pieces of my favourite Fry's Chocolate Cream.

"Wiggle your fingers," the surgeon told me, and I saw tendons covered in blood that stretched and writhed.

"That's how close you came to doing really serious damage," he said.

Deftly, he put six stitches in my right wrist and closed the surface of the wound. Years later, while looking up my father's name on the Internet, I found out that Epsom Hospital was where he had died.

Perhaps this explains my mother's strange confusion and the emotional storm in her brain that, even now, won't correct itself. Despite my showing her the scars on the backs of my hands, and even thought it makes no sense to believe that I cut my wrist when she knows I put it through a window, the horrific fantasy won't leave her mind. Somehow, she has fused the two stories into an ugly lie.

Although these events are long behind us, they tend to re-surface when my mother gets anxious, as if anxiety triggers that particular portion of her brain where the memories are stored. After her hyper manic episode in 2006, she visited my brother, Richard, in Australia, and the stress brought on a brief relapse. Perhaps it had been too soon to travel, or the intense heat and light of Australia, coupled with a change in routine, was just too much.

As she slipped back into rapid cycles of worrying, this old story about my hand-cutting emerged while we were speaking on the telephone one day. It was a painfully one-sided conversation. She had begun by describing her room, the location of other people in the house, and her futile attempts at ironing. As she spoke, she was pacing the room, and I pictured her like a small caged animal going from wall to window and back again. In the brief pauses amidst her rapid-fire conversation, I could hear the sounds of my young nephews in the background, playing.

"What if I don't get better?" she had said. "What if they have to put me in some institution? What if I never make it home?"

There was no time to reassure her, before she launched into fears about how she *would* get home and about the plans my brother was making.

"I don't want to disrupt anyone. I don't want people knowing. What will they say in the village if I come home before the allotted time? They are all talking about me. If you hear any plans, please tell me. Now I must take my medication. I can go a little over the dosage, right? My doctor tells me that people with severe anxiety have a dosage that is ten times greater than mine."

"I am sure it is fine, Mum."

"Can I quote you on that if anyone asks?"

"Of course."

"Am I worse than last time?"

"Not worse. It's not as intense as last time. Do you know what triggered it?"

"Total lack of communication. This house is so big. People speak to me without turning their heads; I can't hear them. I don't know what people are thinking. I don't want to be a burden. I'm staying in my room. I have things to sort out and throw away."

Then, quite suddenly, she skipped tracks and fell deeply into the past. First, she was at a cricket match at my brother's preparatory school, and Hubert had come as a stand-in surrogate father. She felt that my uncle was being aloof with Michael who was eager and shy. Another shift, and she was deep in memories of my father, and then, quite abruptly, we landed at my boarding school.

Up until then, I had been a somewhat distant observer, listening to her stories without getting pulled into the drama. But when she spoke of me hurting myself, young Julia crawled out from under the debris of childhood and stood defiantly with hands on hips. Now I was caught: my desire to set the record straight, and my need to be understood, trumped common sense.

"But I never tried to hurt myself by cutting my wrists," I told her.

"That is not true," she said. She rushed into the story of the man who told her that I was hiding my hands with my long sleeves; he had condemned her for not noticing, and his words had cut deep.

"Mum, don't you want to know what really happened?" I said sharply.

"I know what happened," she replied. "My friend will corroborate."

She had repeated her story to friends; they had sat around and discussed me. Now she was presenting these "witnesses" as if fabricated stories had more validity than the truth. She had stolen my story and re-written my past.

"I was so worried," she continued in a rush. "I had just told you about your father's suicide a short while before. Your words produced such guilt in me. You said, 'why couldn't we have saved him?'"

These memories filter back as we sit in the pub, circling the past even as we speak about the present. There is nothing more that I can do. After my mother's return from Australia, I wrote her a letter calmly detailing the incident on the balcony, calmly reiterating that I only ever cut the backs of my hands, and calmly requesting that she accept the truth and no longer tell false stories about me. It had a limited effect. For a short while, the truth took hold, as if the facts had rearranged themselves. But then the old story resumed its familiar course.

Perhaps it was her way of showing that she understood my anguish; or, perhaps, more simply, it was a distorted expression of her own unnecessary guilt. It no longer matters as much. What matters more is that I know; I am writing it all down, so that I know the truth.

The truth now is different from the truth then. As a teenager, I had no words for the deadening effect of school or the disorientation that followed in the wake of my mother's revelation about my father's death. She had altered the landscape of my life, changed the parameters and proportion, and then thrust silence on me. Facts that she had had more than a decade to absorb were now assumed into my teenage life as if there was no need for emotional processing. I was denied mourning, or denied a father, for a second time, and then made acutely aware of my mother's feelings.

My mother's guilt and anguish, her unresolved grief over my father's suicide, and her sense of loyalty to him, had left her ill equipped to deal with the emotional fall-out for her children. It is not a criticism. How could she possibly help with our grief if she had not processed her own? When she told the truth about our father, it was the difficulties of *her* life that pressed at the edges of my consciousness and made me push her away. When she latched on to a confused version of the events at my boarding school, and convinced herself that I had tried to do serious harm, the story become one more tragedy for *her* to bear. My sadness only added to a pile of emotional residue that choked her system.

Meanwhile, I exhibited all the signs of an angry, defiant teen, while I mapped my feelings silently with broken glass on small patches of skin. But then she trumped me. She inserted herself into the microscopic world under my control, and she repeated her false imaginings over and over until she had a mental breakdown of sorts. In effect, I had made my mother ill. As a little girl, I was not enough to make my father stay; then, I became too much, capable of sending my mother into a nervous collapse.

12

There's a photograph of my father and brothers standing in a line hunched over cricket bats ready to receive a ball. They are posed identically, crisp figures against the well-tended grass of the fenced-in Brown House batting area. My father is in his late thirties, and Michael and Richard are eight and two. Although the neatness of this image is a conceit of the photographer, they represent a congruent sporting lineage that is unabashedly male.

As a girl coming of cricket playing age in the 1970s, my prowess was largely unexplored. Although I played with my brothers in the back garden, the official sport seemed solely the province of boys. My grandmother, Gramy, was a staunch supporter of these masculine games; apparently, she watched me bowl to my brothers one day, with a style uncannily similar to theirs, and remarked, "Pity she's a girl."

To some extent, "pity she's a girl" was a narrative that ran through parts of our family, shaped by women like my grandmother who both controlled and revered their men. She strongly identified with her sons and grandsons, taking immense pleasure in managing, or being involved in, their social and sporting lives. Cricket, in particular, as the photograph suggests, held an allure. The passing on of skills and talent admitted each new generation of boys into a network of social and cultural ties.

I am less certain of my own lineage, less certain of the inheritances passed to the women in our line. Behind the deferential service to masculine traditions lie endurance, social artistry, unexplored creativity and strength. But these exist outside institutions or ritualistic games. Even though I eventually attended the same school as my brothers for my final two years, it was not a place that helped me develop a set of comfortable values, nor did it immediately link me to the larger world. Instead, boarding school was like a forge that created pressure and discomfort, forcing me to look elsewhere for what mattered.

~

On a warm day in June, some weeks before my mother's angiogram, I visited this boys' boarding school with Michael and Caroline. I was enjoying a short break from the anxieties of home by staying with them in London. We had decided to visit the school because their son, Peter, was playing in a cricket match.

We parked near the boundary and set up camp with deck chairs and rugs close to other parents under the shade of an oak tree. My nephew was on the fielding side, intermittently bowling and then guarding the nearby boundary where Michael could stroll close enough to offer water and fatherly cricketing tips. I watched for a while, enjoying my brother's obvious pride and pleasure in seeing his son play well, and then went off to tour some of the more familiar landmarks from my two-year sojourn there.

It was an intentional tour; I wanted to consciously acknowledge and release certain aspects of my past. My first stop was the chapel, positioned close to the cricket pitch as if it might while away the empty hours in admiration of this gentlemen's game. The building is an architectural triumph, but the interior is cold and, to my mind, does not offer much comfort. Rather, it is the daily venue for conformity and spectacle. Ten minutes or so before the beginning of the mandatory daily service, the quiet lanes of the school fill with jostling bodies erupting out of buildings that seemed empty moments before. Boys are still putting on jackets, hair looks as if it has not been brushed in days, and shirts hang below sweaters as they edge and barge their way towards the great arched doors.

In my day, girls paraded in and out of chapel separately under the watchful eyes of seven hundred boys. We were not yet well integrated - more like cream skimming the dark hot surface of the school. The current girls, the ones I had seen at least, appear more composed and comfortable and they wear a uniform of sorts. Back then, as an awkward sixteen-year-old half-hidden in baggy clothes, walking out of chapel had been excruciating; the different parts of my body had seemed to work independently with no central core.

On this day, when I pressed my head against the chapel's wooden door and took hold of the metal handle, it turned helplessly in my hands; the chapel was shut. For a few moments, I stood there and let scenes from the past crowd my mind; the sixteen-year-old certainly deserved love and compassion. School had not been easy, and there were tests of reputation at every turn. Each night, for instance, we had to be walked home to our lodgings by a boy - an ironic practice, since it encouraged wayward behaviour and placed huge pressure on girls. We were judged either way, scrutinized for being too frigid or too loose.

Next to the chapel, a stretch of immaculate grass looked ready for bowling; behind it, the mysterious building with the faux battlements reserved for masters arched over the back road exit as if preventing escape. In the early eighties, men made up almost the entire teaching staff, but women have now breached these walls. I am not one of them. Despite occasional invitations from the alumni associations, or my brothers' cricketing friends, I have never been inside this building. For me, the place symbolizes an inauthentic line between masters and pupils – one that was carelessly monitored in my day when there were frequent crossings. Entering the building now would seem duplicitous, as if I were party to a cover-up or an elaborate charade.

In all fairness, I think the masters needed orienting to co-education as much as we did. Even the ones who did not step over the teacher/student boundary into intimate relationships struggled to find ways to deal with girls. My report cards were often riddled with gender stereotypes. My housemaster, not content with commenting on my academic and sporting prowess, praised my ability to "marry drive and charm in a wholly admirable way."

This curious statement refers to the end of my time at this school rather than the beginning. When I first arrived in the fall of 1979, insulated from feeling as if painted with a layer of resin, I did not garner such glowing reports. My rebellious nature, expressed through scruffy dress and too much socializing, ensured cautionary remarks. At the end of the first term, my history teacher, a stumpy individual who clenched the stem of his well-used pipe and breathed alcohol on you, commented that, "my squires had proved a distraction." By my second term, my housemaster had labelled me "truculent" and complained about my tendency to "mix with the lads." According to him, I wrote-off anything that didn't go my way and this gave a "slightly sour edge to relations with authority."

Past the masters' enclave and the great hall, where the whole school still gathers for occasional assemblies, a network of paths leads to the classrooms. Some of these were the same draughty, ornate stone buildings I remembered, but a smattering of pre-fabricated additions suggested that the school was either short of funds or growing rapidly.

At one of the classrooms windows, set on a level with the path and sheltered by an arched corridor, I stopped to imagine myself as a seventeen-year-old. I had shoulder-length hair back then, and I could remember sitting in this classroom in black jeans and winkle-picker boots nonchalantly strumming a guitar. My songs were intended for the teacher who flirted with me during lessons and whose classroom was conveniently located nearby. On this particular day, he had parked his small foreign car around the corner; as he walked back towards the classrooms, he saw me. With his arms full of books and his heart quite empty, he had stopped to talk and to initiate our affair. The window came to symbolize whatever threshold we had crossed.

It seems crazy now that an affair was even possible. The buildings were exposed and the grounds laid out under watchful eyes, while the roads in and out of the school were easily monitored. Either there were no watchful eyes in those days or no sensitivity to the appetites of masters and pupils. Or perhaps things were known but not spoken of, or spoken of but not taken seriously.

Whatever the case, an affair was bound to end in pain and confusion for at least one of the people involved, and the teacher was far more experienced and cynical than me. Once, I asked him if he had ever done this kind of thing before. He had sat back, cool and collected in his white shirt, blue jeans and Doc Marten boots. He had watched me for a while in silence and then smiled slowly.

"What do you think?" he had asked.

I did not answer, and the silence had filled with my doubt and longing. He had avoided the truth, and I was free to fill in the blank in any way I needed. Looking back now, I see that he was a skilled seducer. He had been weaned in the sixties, and he wrote poetry that perfectly touched my desire for expression and freedom; and although he taught in a public school, he identified as working class and he used his difference as a kind of sex appeal. His wiles had landed in fertile ground. He had already asked the kinds of questions that haunted me and induced boredom in most of my friends; seventeen-year-olds were not typically concerned with the meaning of life.

It is galling now to remember how badly I wanted approval and recognition and how deeply I longed for some purpose in life. The only real warmth at school had come from the chaotic host family where I lodged. My roommate, Alex, was vaguely punk, and we moved in different circles, both assuming the other was more confident and popular than we were. In actuality, we struggled in an environment solely geared to boys. The closest thing to guidance were chats with our landlady who would give us homemade bread fresh from the oven and showed us how to milk the family goat; she offered us a relaxed affection as easily as she showered her own children with love. But it was never enough.

Now, I can trace a path from my father's death, through a thicket of confused fumbling with my brothers, and into the hands of men who were emotionally cut off. I was searching for male approval; I wanted to feel special and chosen, and it seemed as if that always came at a price. For in trying to fill the hole left by my father, I became vulnerable to other people's desires and remained temporarily ignorant about my own. Small recurring signs of my attraction to women had no place in which to flourish.

The first time I had slept with a boy, at seventeen, it was mostly an effort to deflate the pressures of expectation. The actual experience had been disappointing, like starting a book with fresh hopes then finding you had already read it. Similarly, sex with the teacher was disappointing, after the initial thrill of sneaking into the back seat of his car or meeting in secluded woods. It was being wanted, and wanting in return, that held the real power; the actual physical proximity of bodies proved surprisingly disconnecting.

When school had ended, and I had distractedly scraped through my exams, I left for a summer trip through Europe and then Egypt. Distanced from my friends by headphones that fed me snippets of my lover reading from *The Wasteland* and recordings of his favourite songs, the trip unfolded in a series of discordant encounters: a Canadian-Italian man who feigned friendship and tried to serve us up to his local friends; a young Belgian, drying out in Athens from his heroin addiction, who shattered the glass he held too tightly in a café one afternoon; a taxi driver who abandoned us at the pyramids near Cairo when we refused his outrageous additional charges. In essence, the trip mirrored my disconnected inner state. But when I returned home, heavy and eager with expectation, the teacher unceremoniously dumped me.

All this came back as I stood near the window - flashes of the past at odds with the languid passivity of the afternoon. The arched corridor felt thick with memories, as if they needed my permission to disperse. Weeks or months after the teacher delivered his verdict, he had sent a card. He had drawn a picture of the open window, this window, and asked if we could meet again. He wanted sex without any emotional involvement – no strings of any kind. This cynical offer was perhaps his one true gift; he made it much easier for me to walk away.

After the affair, there had been a sudden emptiness, a vacuum, as if a trapdoor had opened and I had tumbled back into my life. Euphoria and longing had been difficult houseguests, and they had left a mess behind. I rallied for one more term at school, a failed attempt at Oxbridge, and then secured two places at solid universities in the north. I thought a change of scene and culture would do the trick. But it had all felt meaningless. People lived on the surface, it seemed, worrying about appearances and accepting things as they were because it was easier to settle than make waves. Staying in this environment would have meant the end of hope.

As I stood at the window in my adult body, eyes closed and one hand lightly touching the stone of the window ledge, I acknowledged the past without fanfare. Pages of my life turned in rapid succession as I embraced the girl I was and the woman I had become.

Back towards the playing fields, I trod softly over cropped grass and flagstones warmed in the afternoon sun. I slipped my shoes off, feeling pleasurably sacrilegious as I wandered past the statue of the school's august founder in my bare feet.

The cricket had temporarily ceased; white figures ambled towards the pavilion for mounds of sandwiches and milky tea. Up the creaking wooden stairs, shoes on and wings furled, I saw my nephew with grass stains on his knees. Behind him, my brother was talking cricket with some old boys, as if there was nowhere else he would rather be.

One of the men, older than Michael, engaged me in conversation laced with awkward gallantry and innuendo. He pretended that I was a delicious family secret, kept under wraps, and he pressed me for information about boyfriends or husbands.

"I date women," I told him, baldly and without hesitation, his presumption having made this easy. He shifted visibly back, and his face crumpled in doubt for just a moment. He regrouped quickly and then glanced up and down my body as if he were accessing a property.

"What a loss," he said. "Well, whatever makes you happy, I suppose." Then he raised his voice a little, just above the sound of the teacups that clinked in polite unison, and proceeded to lament the introduction of girls to the school.

"I wouldn't have liked it," he said, explaining how women with large breasts - he stared at me as he said this - would have distracted him as an adolescent boy. He did not use the word "breasts" of course; he called them "tits" and he cupped his hands provocatively. There was anger at the edge of him, as if my sexuality was a personal affront.

"How long was your last relationship?" he suddenly asked, with no apparent connection to his previous comment. His face was red and his manner insinuating, as if we were drinking in a bar. It seemed that he wanted to stamp me as illegitimate – not the delicious family secret he had imagined at all.

If my mother had been there, she would have urged a polite response. She has a blind spot - a tendency to defer to men. She was the one, after all, who had sent me as a surrogate to Portugal at age sixteen when my brother's girlfriend had dumped him. Or perhaps he had dumped her. At any rate, Michael and I drank Cinzano on the balcony of our shared hotel room, and all week long, the hotel staff mistook us for husband and wife. Certainly, my mother would have expected me to answer this man's question with a smile. But I felt cold and antagonistic, and I stared him down in silence. In this dimly lit pavilion among the cricket whites, fish-paste sandwiches, and small sickly cakes, the dark underbelly of the school seemed alive and well.

I made my last visit to this school on leavers' day, just a week later, when the grounds were abuzz with parents swapping stories about their children's achievements and hoards of people sipping champagne in small white tents. Behind the monastic looking buildings, arrow-shaped signs pointed to different exhibits, and a classy looking portable toilet with wooden and brass fixtures announced itself as 'The Royal Flush.'

In the art building, tucked at the back of the school, youthful talent revealed itself through trees etched on glass, brooding self-portraits, and cartoon animations cavorting on small screens. The rooms hummed with murmured praise as if a small choir were hidden in its rafters. One girl steered her mother past impressionist paintings she, the parent, deemed "not art" and showed her a cluster of reassuringly realist depictions of the school and the grounds.

Near the studio, the technology building was empty. A line of plastic swivel chairs sat idle in front of computers, and, at the far end of the room, a large screen showed an endless loop promotional video. It was well produced, slick, a tempting piece of propaganda focused on the boys' experience in academics, sport, music, and theatre. The girls made only brief appearances, usually to articulate the beneficial effect a female presence had on their male cohorts.

When I returned to watch the cricket, where my brother and nephew were playing on opposing teams, most of the parents had set up elaborate picnic tables. There were full meals laid out under awnings, and the wine flowed freely; an air of excited nostalgia hung over the event.

"It's paradise, isn't it?" one father said, referring to the school and facilities with an expansive sweep of his arm.

"Well, it may be for some, but not all," I ventured. He looked puzzled but conceded the point.

As the day wore on, I felt my distance from the school, from the rituals playing out on the green lawns, and from the assumptions about what constituted a life. The day hung heavy, and in the background a faint worry about my mother protruded. She was coming to join us, and she had sounded agitated on the phone. When her stocky figure finally came into view, she marched across the grass in short, sharp steps and waved in the direction of her grandson who was bowling - a *faux pas* she would never have committed in a regular state of mind.

Yet despite this inauspicious beginning, there had been no other glaring oddities as the day wore on. If anything, I was the one who was agitated. By the time we had visited the long white tent filled with old men in striped blazers eating egg sandwiches and drinking muddy tea in plastic cups, it was all too much. I had no more patience for bat against ball, the click of the scoreboard, the polite claps and murmurs of spectators, or the white figures moving slowly around the green. I perched on the edge of my seat, fingering the car keys until my mother got the hint. I did not belong in the lineage of cricket; I was only ever a spectator there.

PART TWO
DEPARTURE

13

A NECESSARY FREEDOM

When I left England at eighteen it was an act of self-love. Fresh out of boarding school, a privilege that had left me unmoored, as if this rarefied world had unset my co-ordinates, I had been relying on rebellion and resistance to fuel my passage. It had worked for a while, but underneath it was a sharp longing to feel the significance of my life. Family dynamics set in motion by my father's suicide had absorbed too much of my available energy. I had lurched between need and self-protection without finding a steady platform from which to invent a sense of self. I needed a complete break – a new story in fact – in order to begin my life.

There was nothing much in England to hold me. I was living in a bed-sit thirty minutes from home with my cat, Sam, and my Honda 150 motorbike. I had found a temporary waitress job and was essentially waiting for university to begin. Visits home had been reduced to brief encounters, where I strode in with my winkle picker boots and black leather trousers demanding to know if I had any post.

My one secret sliver of hope was a planned six-week adventure to Israel where I would live and work on a kibbutz. I had stumbled on the phenomenon of the kibbutz in my search for alternative ways of living. Although I had no personal knowledge of Israel, and no clear idea of what kibbutz life was like, something in its democratic structure had appealed to me. I had simply applied to an organization that handled volunteer placements and left it up to fate.

When at last I joined the plane that was full of passengers, I knew that on one level I was leaving the past behind. In England, everything I touched was dimmed by the shadow of my father's death and our family history; this adventure was a pure expression of my soul. It was late summer 1982, and I was headed to the Promised Land.

❧

Hebrew chatter fills the air. The sounds are rich guttural utterances that catch in my heart like stray seeds. As the plane taxis into Ben Gurion airport, there is a press of bodies and people strain to get their first glimpse of land; when we disembark, several men crouch on the tarmac and kiss the ground. My throat grows tighter, and there is a sensation of beating wings in my heart as if something is trying to get free.

Inside the airport building, men with jackboots and heavy machine guns stand guard at the exits like pillars on a tomb. Compulsory army service means uniformed men and women are as common as the falafel stands found on most street corners. Still, it will take several weeks before I adjust to this sight and longer to accept the fact that I am travelling in a war zone.

At the main bus terminal, I have my first taste of real falafel choosing toppings from a tempting array of brightly coloured sauces, salads and pickles. In the hot dry air, under the scratch and cry of unknown voices, my adventure begins with a pocket of warm, moist bread and rich sauces that spill over my hand.

The bus goes all the way north to where the kibbutz sits on the eastern shore of the Sea of Galilee. Through the window, the landscape shifts from city to desert to cultivated plot, until we run alongside the water on a road lined with date palms. It feels at once familiar and deliciously strange. The choice of kibbutz had been out of my hands, and fate it seemed had been particularly kind. Despite the huge electric gates, periodic watchtowers, and fences rimmed with barbed wire, the kibbutz feels like a jewel nestled between the hills of the Golan Heights and the sacred water known to Israelis as Lake Kinneret.

At eighteen, I am only dimly aware of the politics that make barbed wire and watchtowers a necessity. It is a fragile area, contested not only because of competing land claims, but because it borders the southwest edge of the Golan Heights; behind these hills lurks Syria. The kibbutz has survived since 1937, and defensive strategies have been as important as the efficient cultivation of the land and the strategic use of the lake's charm and history to attract paying guests.

On first inspection, the kibbutz is comprised of a series of white cinderblock houses and communal gathering spaces set on well-tended lawns. The buildings are interspersed with pathways, rather like an informal college campus or holiday village. Volunteers have their own area near a small clubhouse set up for drinking and parties. My room, shared with an Australian girl called Jo, has a tiled floor, two single beds, a crate for a side-table, and a makeshift set of shelves.

Scattered around the volunteers' buildings, the rest of the kibbutz comprises the dining room, the house where children spend time away from their parents in a communal setting, agricultural and other work buildings, accommodations for full-time residents, and the small shop where we can spend the coupons earned from volunteer work on such things as snack food, toiletries, cigarettes and airmail paper for our letters home.

When the sun goes down on my first day there, the paths fill with people heading to the cafeteria-style dining room for home-cooked food. The evening meal is hot, but during the day there are supplies of kibbutz-grown avocados, peppers, dates and olives, as well as stark white yoghurt that has a tangy, bitter taste.

The volunteers sit in their own section of the dining room, apart from the full-time residents, and on my first night, I join a mixed table. There is Wayne, a muscular American in his thirties who is covered in tattoos; James, a committed Christian visiting from South Africa; and then a cluster of Danes who stand out because of their pale skin and their startling white-blonde hair. People are friendly, but I sense cliques and allegiances formed around cultural similarities or levels of responsibility on the kibbutz. Most people, it seems, have religious or political reasons for being here, and most people are older than me.

After dinner, we sit on the porches outside our rooms making light conversation as the night folds in around us. A slack-jawed, heavy-set Austrian man called Emile, who wears his long hair pulled back in a ponytail, holds forth like a sage.

"You know," he remarks languidly, "you can learn everything you need to know from a tree."

His face is calm and wise, and I want desperately to understand what he means. Compared to some of the other volunteers, who have travelled more widely, my experiences feel limited and parochial. That evening, I am a silent observer, staring at the outlines of trees and half-turned faces, until I turn in for my first night's rest. I sleep fitfully, adjusting to the warm sticky air and the buzz of mosquitoes that have found their way through the screens.

At half-past four the next morning, Jo is already fastening her workbooks, with one foot up on the cinder block that supports the screen door. Her hands, pulling the laces tight then synching them onto the hooks, look strong, and her cut off jeans, frayed at the edges, show off a tan from working outside. She beckons me to follow her. In a scramble of work clothes and boots, I stumble out to the parking area where she has joined a group of people sipping tea on upturned logs. The murmur of voices rises like a sacred chant in the cool air as the body of the kibbutz slowly wakes.

When tea is over, we pile into a tractor and chug out of the main gates, moving steadily along the deserted road and then climbing up towards the hills. The cool air stirs me as if I were a kite, the give in the line answered by the pull and bob of my spirit revelling in this new freedom. We watch the Sea of Galilee grow smaller until it is a shimmering island created by the rising sun.

The tractor pulls off the main road, bumps down a rutted lane and then stops; ahead of us, a vast banana grove stretches away in uniform lines. The work that follows is quiet and satisfying. Adam, a tall, lean man with scruffy beard hands us machetes. He shows us in one smooth motion how to lop off the great bell of purple petals hanging pregnant from each plant. He explains that the amputation stimulates the fruit and stops it putting out a long and wasteful stalk.

"That's how you do it," he says. "Work your way along one line of plants and then start a new line. And watch out for snakes."

The machete feels heavy in my soft hands. I swing. Contact - slice – perfect. The great bulbous end drops to the ground. Next one. Same thing. I move steadily on. Sweat drips from my forehead, and small calluses form on my right palm. Every so often, I pause and feel the sun embrace my body; my awareness absorbs the sky, the other volunteers working around me, and the simple dry brown earth covered with leaves and the swollen, fallen bodies of banana pods.

By noon, I am dirty and tired; the sticky sap has stained my shorts and my hands, and the sun is bearing down. We load up the tractor and drive back down the hillside following the same route that we took in the early hours of the morning. Now the sun is at its height, scorching the earth and making the lake seem like a mirage. I am filled by the morning's work and linked by a delicate sense of belonging that has barely any roots.

Life follows this easy pattern: hard work then relaxation, usually on the banks of the Galilee where we swim, play, talk, and idle until the sun begins to dip below the water. Some afternoons, I walk alone in the tufted foothills of the Golan Heights, surprised by patches of wildflowers and lush grasses growing where streams have forced their way above ground. The air is slow and thick, but the land is wary with stray remnants of burnt-out vehicles and twisted metal shells. It is the land that claims me, offering company and bearing witness to my longing. There is something deep, soft and indefinable that cries out.

Once, on the slope of a hill, where a lone ragged thorn tree shook its bony fingers at the sky, a deer loped past in a graceful three-legged bound, the fourth leg barely touching earth as if he might fly. He disappeared over the crest of a hill, and I followed, copying the movement and covering the ground in long loping strides. We seemed elemental - the deer, the tree, and me - as if we had always been here and always would be.

When I return to the kibbutz after these excursions, the lights and music from the small clubhouse feel alien and tinny. The noise and the alcohol seem out of place, as if the perfect idyll of the kibbutz is tarnished somehow. Still I go there, wanting to make deeper connections among the volunteers. I join in plans for a cross-gendered fancy dress party and write home for my favourite hat, described in my letter as "gangsterish."

My mother duly sends the battered green felt trilby, and on the night of the party, I etch a black moustache on my face and put on a borrowed suit with seventies sunglasses. With my hat at a rakish angle, I stroll into the clubhouse edgy with confidence. But after the first flush of impersonal power has faded, I feel even more alone. Drinking only emphasizes our temporary status and our distance from the real heart of the kibbutz.

One night, escaping the noise and confusion of the clubhouse, I lean against a light pole and stare at the full moon that sits in the sky like a child's drawing.

"Beautiful, eh?" A man with hair lighter than the moon stands close to me with arms crossed. His thick Danish accent makes his moustache rise up when he speaks, and he winces as if words feel awkward in his mouth.

"Why aren't you in there with everyone else?" he asks, pointing to the clubhouse.

"I don't feel like being in all the noise."

He almost smiles. This man, who in the daylight is sarcastic, seems gentler under the moon as if the light has softened him. As we talk, the sounds of the bar recede and the song of crickets seems louder. We speak in low voices, murmurs adding to the harmonies of night, about loneliness and about his estranged wife who is also here on the kibbutz. His pain is a thin insistent echo of mine, and it makes him safe.

"Can I come home with you tonight?"

His face is gentle. He holds me as one might hold a child, his body preventing me from saying more. That is all I want really, this feeling of being held. Only I want it to continue all through the night.

"I can't be with anyone," he whispers. "I am still in love with my wife. I don't trust myself, and we are both too vulnerable."

Even his moustache, hard and fine, seems sad and his cheeks are sharp angles. He leaves me there, leaning against the light pole, and walks away; I watch his tired back and rounded shoulders recede until the night swallows him. He has touched a space of unarticulated longing, a raw nerve that dangles loose; he has stirred my unmet desire for love.

As if awakened, days later I am drawn to the edges of a circle gathered around a newcomer – a woman who lounges on a low-slung deckchair.

"Who is she?" I whisper to one of the other volunteers.

"She's travelling around Israel. She is just here for one night to visit a friend. I don't know her name."

The woman is beautiful. She commands the circle of bodies, her voice caressing them, and her pebble-green eyes turn gold in the flickering light from the fire. I sit silently watching, and then she looks at me above the heads of the others and smiles. It is unmistakable. The look and the smile linger.

My body feels as if tiny pins of fire are pricking me all over. She has recognized me, and I have responded with a clear feeling of attraction. Earlier moments, brief experiences in boarding school, now make sense; this is not entirely unknown just never fully explored. Pleasure runs through me in a shock; the message from my body is pure and direct.

As the night moves in, the edges of the circle grow more ragged; lingering bodies slowly depart, until we are the only two remaining. She beckons me closer.

"So," she says.

We laugh and gaze at each other. My breath seems trapped somewhere under my ribs, and pressure mounts around my heart. If something does not happen, I might scream into the quiet of this night. But then she finds out my age, and she shakes her head.

"You are too young. I am twenty-eight, and this is your first time."

I try to talk her out of this position, but she is adamant; she is kind and gentle too. When I leave her, quiet and mysterious in the dying light of the fire, I feel as if the embers of that fire are glowing in my heart. A brief but true encounter with a nameless stranger has illuminated the path of my desire. Now, I know where to find my pleasure; now, I know where to look.

It would have been impossible to have such clarity back home in England. There, I was too hemmed in by tradition and expectation, as if someone had pre-told my story. Here on the kibbutz, in a foreign country, life seemed to unfold more honestly moment by moment.

It was the following evening when I saw Michal. She must have been there each night, quietly wiping down the tables in the dining room after meals, absorbed and serious with her full, generous profile turned down towards her work. But on this day, she looked up and something passed between us. Later, she would tell me that she spilled the water she was carrying and missed the container when she tried to rinse out her cloth. The next night, when she was serving food in the dining room, she looked directly into my eyes.

"Do you want some?" she asked, indicating the food in front of her, but also smiling slightly.

I nodded and took the food, but I also took in her face, her dark curly hair, the mole near her mouth, and the dimple in her left cheek.

14

"You were not in my plan," Michal tells me recently, when I trace her through a website for former volunteers. "I was ready to meet boys and think about marriage and children not fall in love with a woman again."

We have not seen each other for a quarter of a century, although she has searched for me and our paths have almost crossed in America several times. We laugh when we speak; her thick accent, the childlike gasps of delight, the throaty merriment are so familiar they seem to come from inside me.

It is her face I see when I remember Israel, her fingers cracking open a pomegranate, and her lips pressed into the tender flesh of a persimmon. She is a thread that connects me, or a note of music that brings me back to my essential sound.

"Remember when I came over to your room and introduced myself?"

"No," she corrects. "You climbed a tree near my house, and you played your guitar. You sang until I came over. Don't you remember? You sang a soft song. What was it? *Angie*, I think."

"Well, how could you resist that?" I reply.

❧

Neither of us resists, and the sweet intensity of first love works my heart like an accordion. But life is a curious mix of deferral and pleasure. All week, Michal stays in Tel Aviv where she studies music and drama. In her absence, I focus my energies on kibbutz work. Aaron, a stocky Arab man, recruits me for the garden. He lets me drive a tractor and shows me how to fix the black plastic irrigation tubes that run like arteries under the lawns. When I am moved into a supervisor position at the camp and caravan site, trading in tractor for golf cart and walkie-talkie, I miss his cherubic face and his riotous curls. My new job is more demanding. The tourists who rent caravans and come to the restaurant for plates of crisp St. Peter's fish are not always tidy. They leave old food, dirty towels, and numerous stray bottles and cans in their wake.

On weekends, Michal comes home to the kibbutz. Her room is close to the lake and overhung with orange blossoms. It is there, honeyed by fragrance, that we hold and touch, skin to skin, wrapped and unwrapped, her mouth set passionately on mine. When the sun sets in gashes of gold and crimson that bleed into the water, the wavering lines of birds, etched briefly on the red horizon, carry my heart's wishes. Along the shore, a swing-set teases with the possibility of flight. Divine presence feels weightless, a brief moment at the arc of the rise when the seat disappears and hands no longer grip the chains.

Ours is an intimacy of revelation, yet we guard our love from unsympathetic eyes. In letters home, Michal is simply a friend, and on the kibbutz, we make love in the safety of her room and take long walks in the hills. Sometimes, she will strip off her clothes and dance. Exhorting me to join her, she lets the sun and wind play on the surface of her skin. I envy her freedom and hope it is catching.

My initial six-week stay extends. Six months is the maximum length you can be on the kibbutz if you are not Jewish; anything longer than six months requires a commitment of faith. I defer my university place in England and stay for as long as I can.

In a letter home, I ask my mother if she will continue to care for my cat and beg for her understanding: "I don't know when in 1983 I will be back. I need to see and experience more. Please don't worry about me. I just don't feel ready to study yet."

A new plan has formed inside me; it seeds itself when Michal shows me several photographs from her recent visit to India when she stayed at the ashram of a well-know meditation teacher. In one photograph, Michal is standing next to a tall Indian woman in robes; this is the teacher's translator, about to become Guru in her own right. In a second photograph, this same woman is in monk's robes undergoing her initiation ceremonies. It is this photograph that captures my attention.

The woman's head is shaved and tilts disarmingly to one side; three stripes of sacred ash mark her forehead; a circle of red turned grey by the photograph burns between her black brows; an enigmatic smile barely touches her lips. Perhaps it is her gaze that has leached the photograph of its colour. It has that effect on me, as if all the colour and intensity of my life is drawn to this one point of connection, this eye contact between the woman in the photograph and me.

Michal and I laugh about this now; she introduced me to my teacher, and to meditation, but I was the one who went to the ashram and stayed nine years. There was something about the woman in that photograph that captured me, and I had an immediate and deep desire to know her. It did not feel strange or outlandish; it felt as if I had made a clear and compelling choice from within. Without the voices of family, or painful reminders of the past, I was now making choices that originated from a deeper, more instinctual place inside.

In spite of my feelings for Michal, I begin to make small trips away from the kibbutz in preparation for my inevitable departure and for a peeling away of my heart. Sometimes, I venture to Tiberius across the water or to one of the other local communities nearby. One afternoon, I hitch a ride home with volunteers from another kibbutz. The driver, a middle-aged man with bushy beard, tells us in broken English that he grew up on a nearby kibbutz and is returning home from military service. He seems friendly and safe; assumptions pass between us as easily as handshakes.

When the others are dropped off, and I am the only one left in the van, the mood shifts. He drives for a while in silence and then abruptly turns left down a side road.

"Where are you going?" I ask, trying to sound calm.

"I just need to do something," he replies, staring ahead at the road.

The van rocks from side-to-side as we jolt over dry ground rutted with tractor marks. Once, when I was a little girl, a man followed me in a French arcade. Richard, only two years older than me, scared him off, but the man's nervous, fleshy face haunted my dreams for days.

We stop abruptly at the edge of a banana grove. It is dusk, and all I can see behind the hard outline of the man's face, half-turned towards me, are the bulbous tips of banana pods pendulous and dark. He gestures to an old mattress rolled up in the far corner of the van. It is white with dark blue stripes. The nail on the man's forefinger is several inches long.

"Take me to the kibbutz right now," I yell.

His hand slams against the steering wheel, and he mutters in Hebrew looking back at me with the whites of his eyes. Then he shoves the driver's door open and gets out. I don't know whether to make a run for it or stay sitting in the back seat. Is he coming round to my side? The moment stretches thin. I hear his belt buckle hit the side of the van. Then his zipper opens with a sound like metal rain. I catch a glimpse of him through the open door; he is jerking himself off in sharp, angry bursts.

He finishes, gets back into the van, wipes his hand on an old rag, and then reverses quickly back up the dusty path. At the highway, he swings the van around and shoots forward; we careen into the night like fools. Dust from the road mingles with the scent of his body, and I bite down on my fear. When he screeches to a halt near the kibbutz, engine gunning, I leap out and slam the door behind me in my only possible gesture of rage. My heart beats a staccato rhythm; I could so easily have been raped.

Israel itself has this primal quality: beauty and danger live side by side. On a trip with other volunteers to the Lebanese border, the vast horizon is filled with the muted drumming of distant shells, and the hillsides are blemished with the residue of war. We drive on long, lonely highways carved through rock and shimmering desert, and we camp at night in the fragrant hills. We make fires, cook our own food, and listen to the distant wail of animals as we delay sleep and the nightlong assault of the dive-bombing mosquitoes.

When I travel to the bigger cities, I go alone. Jerusalem, carved from swamps and desert, is another world entirely from the hearty simplicity of kibbutz life. Inside the ancient city walls, Arab markets resound with life. Tourists, mesmerized by noise and colour, finger the leather belts, scarves, and decorated purses while the merchants haggle; in pursuit of sales, they send sweet tea dancing from the spouts of elegant samovars and offer up plates of humus drizzled in olive oil and sprinkled with pine nuts. All this life, while in another part of the city, figures in dark suits and wide brimmed hats press heads against the Wailing Wall and tuck prayers into its crevices.

Israel beckons and excludes; it is a place of contrasts where the passions of different groups collide. On Christmas Eve in Bethlehem, the crowds surge towards the Church of the Nativity, forcing a way in the name of the Prince of Peace. But away from the noise and competition, a group gathers around a fire in an open field. Light flickers across the faces of children and animals pressed close to the warmth, while men and women chant softly in unfamiliar Slavic tones. Far away in Nazareth, people fall asleep on rooftops pressed against the stars.

Although I left Israel, she has never left me. All these years later, I can picture the moment when the bus pulled out of the kibbutz parking lot and took me away for the last time. As we rumbled down the dusty path towards the exit, I craned my neck to catch a last glimpse of Michal. She stood there, one hand raised, getting smaller and smaller like the Russian dolls hidden inside each other in perfect miniature replicas. And then the bus plunged out of the gate, and we turned onto the main highway, heading south and then west to the port city of Haifa.

Heartache reduced my journey across the Mediterranean Sea to a faint pastel of warm breezes, the boat's engine throb, and the distant comfort of other backpackers making their temporary home on the wooden deck. Now that such crossings are rare, I wish I could remember the lonely thrill of standing under the night sky listening to the water slip past the prow of the boat and searching for the eerie outline of land.

The boat must have been a ferry, and I suppose it might have travelled via Cyprus to a suburb of Athens called Piraeus. This was the usual route for people, like me, who went to Athens in search of cheap airline tickets. When I arrived there in early January 1983, it seemed, at first, like a modern city crammed with fashion boutiques and cut-price travel agencies; everywhere I went, there were backpackers with heads buried in maps. But further in, the city became a series of market squares, corner churches and cobbled alleys; in these quieter streets, Orthodox priests strode by in sombre robes, women in headscarves transported their wares to sell, and younger men idled away time in cafés and bars.

From Athens, I sent a rather lurid postcard home: a Greek maiden holds up an urn, perhaps praising its beauty, while a Greek soldier stands awkwardly with his spear and shield; he is gazing at her and shows no interest in the urn at all. The postcard lets my mother know that I am still alive, waiting for a flight to India, and working in a donut shop in exchange for lodging. I doubt that this eases her mind.

When I had called from Israel, telling her I was going to India to meet a meditation teacher, there had been a long silence at the other end of the line. She had struggled to find pertinent questions. Since Gramy had recently died and left her grandchildren some money, she knew I was not asking permission or seeking approval. Perhaps it was this freedom that scared her.

Days passed as I languished in the donut shop, eating pastries and watching the busy street outside. Athens had quickly become stale, and my free lodging at the top of a tall building was plagued by damp. I mourned the absence of hills and trees and pictured the ashram as a haven of peace and discipline. At last, on January 11, 1983, I left Athens and flew to Bombay, India, with only a vague idea of where to find the ashram and a great deal of trust.

15

SACRED GROUND

Two dusty brown children tug on my hands.

"Rupees, Mumma, you have rupees for me, please. Two rupees only, please."

I shake my head, shake off the clinging fingers, and eye the older man on crutches ambling forward to where I stand: western girl, just off the plane, rucksack on her back, guitar under one arm. Nearby, a jumble of black taxis idle their engines and honk their horns. The beggars swarm: gaggles of ragged children with wide grins and eager hands.

I tell one taxi driver my destination; he shakes his head.

"Too far, Madam. Sorry, this taxi only goes into town."

Haggling gets me nowhere, and the crowd around me grows. The heat and the press of bodies foment unfamiliar human and animal smells. To my left, a tall European man with backpack emerges from the doors under the Bombay airport sign. We strike up a conversation, two strangers in a strange land, and I decide to share a taxi with him into town. He carries himself with German efficiency and self-confidence, and he assures me that finding transport will be easier in the centre of Bombay.

We get into one of the idling taxis and drive into the dusk past eerily scarred landscapes scattered with sections of pipe, concrete towers, and bamboo scaffold held together by rope; everywhere there is the casual sight of squatting behinds. The ride is perilous. There are no clear rules on the road, and driving seems to be a noisy test of faith and ingenuity. As we draw closer to the city, rows of shops with bright signs replace the half-built buildings, and the pavements teem with skinny men in polyester trousers holding hands; dotted among the men, groups of girls and women are colourful in their saris and salwar kameez.

The taxi drops us near the centre of town. Hans is a seasoned traveller and takes the lead in finding us a place to stay. He is seasoned, but cheap. We walk for hours past families tucked into the scant comfort of abandoned construction pipes or gathered around fires. Crazy cardboard dwellings with corrugated metal roofs provide minimum cover for people or belongings. We pass one lifeless body left under a white sheet and waiting for someone to take it away.

At last, on a street we have traversed several times, Hans makes a decision. We enter the busy reception area of a large guesthouse that resounds with blaring radios, slamming doors, and shouts in Hindi and Marathi that echo down the halls. A shared room with several beds costs minimal rupees, but it is also open to spectators who come in and out during the night. Doors open and close, radios get loud then soft, giggles and murmurs filter through my consciousness until, finally, my tired body falls into sleep.

When I awake, Hans is already dressed and moving to the door. His tour guide duty is over, and all he offers is a tossed sideways suggestion that I go to the main train station and find a map. It is good advice.

A short while later, the imperial train station is easy to find; it is a vast colonial behemoth packed tight with travellers clutching plastic bags or battered suitcases held together with string. At the map stand, a crude drawing shows my destination. It is at least three hours away to the north: a country outpost among rural villages, marked as a place of pilgrimage and shown on the map as a hand-drawn cluster of temples.

As I stare at these spidery lines, jostled by the horde of train travellers, a thin Indian man coughs politely at my side; with delicacy, he offers himself as my guide.

"Very good. I can take you almost all the way," he says, with that characteristic sideways motion of the head. "I have a German wife at home; you can trust me."

He leads me through the crush of people, and we reach a platform just as a train pulls in. Bodies multiply, as if they had been hiding underground, and the entire train swarms with human flesh. Nothing is left empty: seats, roofs, sides and available rails on the outside of the train are all taken. From above, it must appear as a seething mass of arms and legs.

We push our way into a compartment and sit close together in one seat. People stare, since women generally travel in a separate compartment from the men. As we lurch and sway, pressed by the warm flesh of surrounding bodies, my guide asks about my travels and offers advice about "must see" places he recommends. Hopefully, since I can see nothing beyond the flesh of my travelling companions, the scenes outside the window do not fall into this category.

The train disgorges us at a rural station. Here, I will catch a bus and my guide will return home to his German wife. He escorts me to the right stop, tells the driver I am getting off at the ashram, and gratefully accepts a large pile of rupees. He waves, and then I am lost among the throng of villagers boarding the bus with baskets of fruit, vegetables, spices and salted fish balanced on their heads. When I find a seat, I look back down the aisle and notice that all the villagers have bare feet, dusty and calloused from frequent outdoor use.

The bus is old with no springs left in her hide, and each hole in the road jars the vertebrae in my spine. I sit forward, tipping the seat edge, and look out of the window at the lush rice fields, the oxen pulling carts, and the tall women with picks and shovels working on the roads. In villages where the bus slows or stops, sacred cows amble undisturbed among the women selling vegetables and vagrant dogs lie, sharp-ribbed, in the shade between the homes. Children play games with sticks, stones and discarded rubber tyres.

After some time, we pass a field dotted with men in white dhotis carrying small metal cans, and then a long wall appears that is cleaner than the rest of its surroundings. The driver pulls up in front of a series of buildings tiered like a wedding cake and topped with a golden dome. He points and lets me know that I have arrived. No one else gets off.

Behind me, a lone restaurant does a desultory trade in afternoon chai, and a vendor of garlands, coconuts and kumkum powder nods sleepily at his stall. In the centre of the ashram wall, arched gates fan out from a painted lotus flower with the name of the ashram shaped inside. Through the gates, steps lead directly to a small temple and beyond that a wide courtyard, glimpsed through two open doors.

It is the time for afternoon prayer when I arrive, and the temple has just stirred to life. I stand in the doorway and watch two men, draped in orange, swing their ornate silver-tufted prayers sticks like undernourished majorettes. A strong smell of incense wafts to the outer courtyard, overtaken by the smoky richness of melted ghee. When the men lift trays of lighted wicks, a cacophony of conch shells, horns, and drums erupts and then crescendos. When the sound stops abruptly, the silence hums until a small group of devotees begins to chant. The object of their homage, a large shimmering bronze statue draped with flowers, sits serenely on his plinth in full-lotus pose.

Is it strange to say that all this felt familiar? I was at home in the ashram from the moment I stepped inside. If the welcoming committee was surprised that I had never met the Guru or attended a program of any kind, they seemed to understand how a photograph of her could produce such a response. I was given a brief tour of the ashram and a booklet explaining the *dharma* or rules. Rent would cover my lodging and vegetarian meals in the Indian dining room, and in return, I would do whatever ashram work, or *seva*, I was assigned. There was a schedule of chanting, meditation and selfless service that guests and devotees must adhere to, and strict prohibitions on intoxicants of any kind. With these guidelines firmly imbibed, I could join the several hundred devotees who lived in the ashram full-time.

During the first two days, I was free to wander the ashram and acclimatize to early morning meditation and a series of chants and other practices that imbued the hours with a shimmering presence; here, at last, was an answer to the surface, cursory life at home. Enlivened ritual practice had tangible effects on the body and mind. One only had to breathe the air; everything, from the beautiful gardens to the silent temples, underground halls, or wide magical courtyard was saturated with the energy of spiritual practice.

Perhaps because I adjusted so quickly, it did not seem strange to me that most of the people living in the ashram came from America, Australia or Europe. Indians, I was told, tended to come on weekends and special holidays when large tent cities were erected in the grounds. At other times, they were busy with family life and their cultural mores did not allow for the kind of leisure that a prolonged stay in the ashram required. So, the faces lined up in the communal dining room at lunchtime, where we sat on the floor and ate with the fingers of our right hand, tended to be western and almost universally white. Yet despite the fact that we were adopting customs from another land, the feeling that these customs evoked was universal and intimate. As the servers walked among us at lunchtime, for instance, carrying bowls of rice, dhal, vegetables, and chapattis, their selfless service accompanied by our soft chanting turned a daily need into a shared act of reverence.

On the third day, I am assigned the service of chopping vegetables in the ashram restaurant that offers an alternative to Indian food and does a brisk trade in breakfasts and dinners. Work begins early, before devotees gather for five o'clock chai, and I relish the quiet of the morning when the only sound is the tapping of knives on boards. Work gives focus to the day, and I am easily swept into the mesmerizing precision of slivering onions and chopping potatoes into one-inch cubes.

The Guru is in residence, but so far, I have only caught glimpses of her in the gardens or the courtyard where she sometimes sits. There is an air of suspended anticipation associated with possible sightings of her. One week into my stay, anticipation becomes an excited buzz. Apparently, the elusive woman in the photograph is going to appear at an evening program. We are lifted by this promise, as if doors and windows have been flung open and a fresh breeze has quickened. We try not to hurry through our service, but everyone wants to get a good seat in the hall. By late afternoon, a line has formed in the courtyard, and the bustle of musicians, seating monitors and various technicians passing in and out of the hall intensifies. People are dressed up, I notice, glancing down at my own shirt and jeans.

99

When I enter the underground hall, it is dimly lit and soft with the now familiar scent of incense and the gentle hum of an air conditioner. A hostess looms out of the darkness, the soft silk of her sari brushing her toes as she walks. She beckons me over to the women's side. The carpet feels cool, almost damp, under my bare feet, and I'm grateful for the shawl and the woollen mat, known as an *asana,* that I have purchased at the bookshop; these will help keep me warm and mark off my small territory. For the hall fills quickly, and the rows of people lined up along the stepped semi-circles of the intimate amphitheatre are densely packed.

A woman pumps the bellows of a harmonium with one hand and runs her fingers across the keys with the other; the small box emits a drone which cues a group of musicians and a chant begins. The room gets darker; my neighbours become eerie shapes swaying like plumed grass. Facing us, the Guru's chair sits empty yet emanates a certain presence. I close my eyes; sound wells up and moves into my chest cavity, warming and rubbing like tiny grains of sand. But my throat is tight; my mouth is ungenerous. It feels strangely intimate to make rich loud sounds.

A splash of light fills the far corner of the hall. At least, I think it does. My eyes have opened suddenly, in time to see a tall figure glide into the room; her saffron robes float like chiffon and brush against the faces of people turned towards her. She pauses at the back altar, touches the wooden sandals that represent the Guru's power, then faces forward and moves slowly down the centre aisle. A ripple passes in her wake like wind through a field as heads sink and hands rise in prayer position. At the chair, she bows deeply and looks up at a large framed photograph of her Guru. In liquid motion, she swivels, ascends the chair, and sweeps her legs up under her with robes settling like quieting waves.

As her thick resonant voice joins the chant, the tightness in my throat unlocks. She calls and we respond; the whole room pulsates in an ecstasy of sound that swells and bursts. The Guru leads us to greater and greater heights. And then suddenly, the chant reaches full pitch and ends; the notes die out, we repeat one more line in slow motion, and then we free-fall into meditation going down, down,

down beyond sound or silence. I am plunged in warm honey and buzzing with the vibration of bees. *I could do this for hours; it is amazing. I'm having an experience.* So says my mind. Thoughts follow thoughts. Gradually, the sensations recede. I try to grip on, and they move further away. My neighbour coughs; the air conditioner hums more loudly; someone in the room makes little shrieks; my legs begin to ache, forcing me to shift my position and hug knees to chest. Meanwhile, the Guru sits motionless in her chair.

At last a bell sounds lightly, the harmonium squeezes back into life, and we chant ourselves out of meditation. The lights in the hall rise, and a man sets up a transparent podium and swivel microphone in front of the Guru's chair. She taps lightly on the microphone, places sheaves of paper on the podium and begins to speak in English tinged with an American drawl; she welcomes us with great respect and love.

As the Guru talks, occasionally looking at her notes but more often directing her gaze around the room, her body lifts from it centre and her words emanate with mellifluous precision. Only her hands seem free, the tapered fingers rising and swooping, and when they rest on the podium, I think of doves.

She finishes her talk, someone introduces *darshan*, and instrumental music floods the room. *Darshan*, I have learned, means being in the presence of the truth; it is a time when we can come forward and meet the Guru. Hostesses stand and invite the room one section at a time in two organized lines. Someone hands the Guru a wand of peacock feathers as a blessing tool. As people step up and bow in front of her, she swats heads and brushes faces. Sometimes, she sets the wand across her knees so that she can lean forward. People linger; some expect a word or two from the master and others have questions. The hostesses do their best to keep the lines moving.

My section is called. The same hostess who ushered me to my seat now expects me to vacate it. Everyone is moving, and the space around me gapes. I act as if I know what I am doing and stay put. *Anyway, it is too late to get up now. Besides, it would feel exposing to bow in front of this woman, and I don't even know her.* Just as I think this, the elegant monk turns her head slowly. As if she can read my thoughts, she looks directly into my eyes. I hold her gaze, but I have been breached. She has ripped through the façade of personality in a glance, exposing the falseness of it, and she stares directly at the truth.

16

"Could I please have a spiritual name?" I ask, unable to discern the Guru's features clearly in the dim evening light. She is sitting comfortably in the courtyard with a small gathering of people, and I am kneeling in front of her, inches from her swaying right foot. Above my head, the stars are barely visible through the mango trees. There is a pause, and my knees grow cold on the marble.

"You come so late," she remarks.

Her voice is rich, resonant, and inflected in a way that is hard to read. *Was she being literal? Was she saying something about the lateness of the hour or how long it had taken me, three weeks, to ask for a name? Or was she saying something more profound about my spiritual path?*

A strange confusion overtakes me in her presence. Ten days ago, the Guru had noticed me in the darshan line. It was a Sunday morning, and she had been sitting in the marble chamber above the meditation hall receiving a stream of visitors from Bombay; the darshan line stretched all the way back into the courtyard, and the air was thick with the scent of jasmine. I had moved forward in a press of people and bowed, lowering my head below my heart to acknowledge the divine inner presence that the outer guru represents. As I was getting up to leave, she had glanced at my now familiar outfit of trousers and shirt. With a slight movement of her hand, she had summoned an attendant who scurried off and returned bearing a red cotton sari with a delicate flower design.

Most people would have understood the implicit message to dress in the sari; I did not. To me, it was a sacred item and something that would adorn my room but not my body. The following Sunday, I was back in the darshan line still wearing my white trousers and blue shirt as if nothing had happened. On that day, the Guru had stopped what she was doing and lifted her free hand into the air, twisting and turning it in a corkscrew motion of inquiry. I had smiled awkwardly, and she had grimaced and waved a languid hand. Two older women had sprung forward and ushered me to the side of the marble hall.

"When she gives you a sari, it's because she wants you to wear it," one of them had said. "Don't worry. We will teach you how to put it on."

They had lent me a slip and a *choli*, the small top that goes underneath, and then wound the red sari around my body with expert hands. They gathered and pinned pleats of the material in front, swept the rest of the sari up across my body, pinned it again at the shoulder, and then let it fall down my back in simple accordion folds. My transformation was complete, and when I returned to darshan the Guru had smiled. The surge of elation I felt on receiving this smile was a giddy sensation of equal parts yearning to understand her and fear that I never would.

A similar thing happens now. Thoughts compete for attention, my subtle intuition is lost, and the silence lengthens. The Guru takes pity on me and reaches over to a card file resting on her side table; she flips through it, stroking the cards with her long fingers as if they were tresses of hair. She considers, picks one, and holds the card out saying the name aloud at the same time. She draws out the syllables "Ga-u-ta-mi," so that the "a" becomes long and the "u" sounds more like "ow." In that simple transference, my heart twists up in my name's melodic sound.

Back at my seat, clutching the small card as if it holds the secrets of the universe, I gaze at her inscrutable face in the shadows. A powerful desire to be like her, to know what she knows, to merge with her in fact, rises in me like an ancient call. When she finally gets up, and slips quietly through a door at the back of the courtyard that leads to her private quarters, my heart pulls as if we are physically connected.

Only then do I turn over the card and read the description: "Gautami - the wife of a sage." More about the sage follows, but I

104

have stopped reading. *Who cares about him? The wife of a sage? What does that mean? Gautami - the wife of a sage. It does not improve with repetition. Why did she give me that? Doesn't it have any other meanings? It sounds horribly mundane.* But the name remains just as it is, unadorned and not giving itself to easy definition. Still, from time to time, I will ask around for better definitions, and I will fondly recall the particular resonance it had when the Guru first said the name.

My letters home do not describe such vagaries, but would my mother please consider calling me by my new name? She will gently decline this honour; Gautami sounds a little too strange, and besides, she cannot think of me as anything other than the child she gave birth to and named. I respect her decision, and so I become two people: Gautami in the ashram and Julia at home. This is a profound division that will haunt me for many years. For now, I bridge the gap with expositions on divine consciousness and Guru's grace. "God is in each of us," I proudly declare in one of my letters, and "Life is the play of God and a manifestation of the Self. I am so incredibly blessed to be with a living master."

How these protestations of faith must have sounded to my family. Even to my ears now, they ring with an idealistic fervour. My mother has kept old audiotapes, messages sent from my family one Christmas and my replies back to them; listening to them more than two decades later is strange. There is already the hint of an American accent three years into ashram life, and everything is "so great" and "so beautiful." Indeed, life does have new meaning since receiving *shaktipat* - the transmission of energy from the Guru that jumpstarts your spiritual path. When she initiated me, I had felt vast, as if my being had stretched to contain the universe, and the wash of unconditional love accompanying her touch had cracked my heart wide open. It is this feeling I wanted to convey to my family, but words without the corresponding experience sounded overblown and puerile.

105

As I listen to family members speaking self-consciously on the audio tape, I picture them gathered around the dining room table at our old home. Michael and Caroline have just had their first baby. He is cautiously proud while she is exuberant; she holds Francesca near the microphone as she breast-feeds, and her words are punctuated by wet suckling sounds. Richard, who has already visited the ashram, pipes in with jokes about the money purse I have sent him; it is just the right size for rupees but not so good for English pounds. Finally, it is my mother's turn, and she comes on the tape in a rush. She describes the festivities of Christmas day and laments my absence in a high- pitched voice.

"Francesca will be christened soon," she tells me. "Seeing her so young is a time you will not want to miss."

It is easy, now, to recognize now the separations already occurring after several years away – the events not shared, the transformations not witnessed, and the new priorities rapidly emerging. But for me, this departure from England, this separation from the narratives of family history, was a necessary freedom. If my family assumed that this was a phase I would outgrow, they did not understand the depth of my quest or the profound nature of my awakening.

When the Guru leaves India mid-year, in a convoy of cars with darkened windows, I vow to myself that when she travels again, I will be with her. She has told those of us who remain behind to focus on our service and meditation. She explains that we have two natures - an original one beyond duality, and a more limited nature mired in worldly attachments. She urges us to do the practices, discover our true nature, and know that our happiness lies within.

Some of us stand and watch long after her car has turned a corner. Small boys with skinny legs have run into the street to grab pieces of the coconut that was smashed to ensure an auspicious journey. Flies gather, and discarded garlands bleed slowly into the dirt. When at last we turn and troop back inside, the ashram feels small and quiet without her.

We turn to our spiritual practices with fervour, but my private diary fills with expressions of missing the Guru and observations about my inadequacy. "It is easy to see perfection in the wild fern," I write. "It is so delicate and perfect. It seems hard to see myself or other people the same way." According to my dairy, the list of my imperfections is long:

- My chanting has been terrible – just opening your mouth isn't enough
- I've judged others on the basis of my own ideas and projections
- I've been impatient
- I've wasted my time idly talking
- I've eaten carelessly
- I've thought proudly that I'd attained something
- I haven't surrendered my will to the Guru's at all

Despite these obstacles, by the time the Guru returns, the discipline, burned deep with longing, has taken root. Snippets in my letters home alarm my mother: "It's quite likely that I'll decide university isn't what I need. It isn't really a decision; I'm just letting things flow naturally. University has become a convention; the best timing for it is individual and cannot be mandated."

With each package of guitar strings, favourite shirts and other sundries that my mother sends, she offers a gently worded inquiry into the possibility of my coming home. Getting me back to England seems her best chance of anchoring me to a reality she understands. But her attempts fail and specific inquiries only elicit confident words. I tell her I am guided by my own inner knowing: "When the time is right things fall into place as long as you are surrendered and open to it."

17

A MOTHER'S LOVE

When my mother comes to India, she travels into the unknown. Several things have motivated her visit. Inquiries about the ashram, using all known contacts to India, have produced little information, and attempts to lure her daughter away with offers of a holiday have come to ground in a flurry of letters, telexes and crossed wires. The final straw is her brother-in-law. Nudged by his wife, who has just read an article in *Good Housekeeping* about a notorious Guru who takes advantage of his disciples, Hubert has threatened to intervene. He wants to come to India and rescue his niece from what he fears might be a potentially dangerous cult. The thought of him descending on the ashram galvanizes my mother into buying a ticket.

"I was tearful when I said goodbye to Michael at the airport," she remembers. "Poor Michael; he looked quite worried. I was so afraid no one would be there to meet me when I landed in Bombay."

My mother arrives on the morning of September 24, 1983 and is met with a blast of humid air and a sudden rush of people; a little boy hangs on her baggage cart demanding a sweetie and then money. When she catches sight of me, waiting next to an ashram taxi, she weeps with relief.

She has recorded these first impressions in a thin blue journal. Inside the back cover, a hand-drawn calendar marks the day she arrived and each successive day until she leaves. She measures the dwindling space between her and England with all the diligence of a prisoner doing hard time.

In a shallow box stuffed into her filing cabinet, my mother still has a collection of sympathetic letters from friends and acquaintances who viewed my being in an ashram as some sort of tragedy for her. Even though she had not turned up any dirt on the ashram, she still thought of it as a strange and alien place. My written instructions on what to bring had probably not helped. In addition to several practical things, I had advised her to get a small cushion and get used to sitting cross-legged on the floor. Apparently, I would not be making concessions for my mother's age or lack of experience. I would expect her to follow the full ashram schedule: "Just plunge in, everything will be fine,"

Perhaps it is a blessing that my mother arrives in the early hours of the morning. Darkness mutes many of the sights she will find distressing, and her first impressions of India are quite benign.

"There are very quiet country roads full of pits and holes," she writes in her diary. "We weave from side to side and pass many tumbledown shanties and stray dogs, cats, and cows. The road is deserted except for big lorries, and we stop at a very dilapidated petrol pump – no sophisticated self-service here. Then we stop again at a big lorry park and wind our way round a veritable forest of these big, high rusty looking lorries. The driver goes off for tea – we wait."

Measuring time will be a theme during her seven long weeks in the ashram. She will keep careful account of soothing hot drinks, meals, garden walks, chanting and meditation sessions, and brief but meaningful conversations with me. But initially, all she notes in her journal is that the ashram is bigger than she imagined and the people are friendly. Any disorientation she feels stems mainly from being in a strange country. A loud bang on her first night startles her into wondering if it is an explosion or a bomb. But it is merely thunder, and my mother gets a taste of the end of monsoon rains.

Her first full day begins well. The ashram seems peaceful, and her breakfast scone, washed down with lemon tea, is familiar and reassuring. It is only when we step outside the ashram that little things start to disturb her. The bank clerks, for instance, are strangely inactive, and the procedure for withdrawing money is arcane.

"We sign two slips," she notes, "and give my passport number;

then, we are given a metal token with the number 'one' on it. After about ten to fifteen minutes wait, the man in a little cabin pings a bell once, and I go and present my token. He pays out the money, and I must check that there is not the slightest tear on a note."

When we leave the bank and explore the smattering of shops around the ashram, we go into a "little wooden shack shop that smells awful." My mother is parched, but she finds the bottled soda water foul. Still, she "sits outside the terrible little shack at a table sipping it through a straw."

If she finds the poverty and the smells of India difficult to stomach, my mother does her best to enter into the spirit of the ashram. She attends the Sanskrit chants, works in the sewing room, eats lunch cross-legged on the dining room floor, and begins meditating regularly in one of the garden temples. And when she meets the Guru for the first time, she is impressed. The Guru has a sweet face, and she gives an impressive talk on ashram discipline.

As the weeks pass, there are subtle shifts in my mother's experience. When she first began work in the sewing department, for instance, she continually had to re-do her blind hemming; now, she was being praised. And her other job washing bottles in the clinic has garnered her a new friend: Sita is a sixty-two-year old Indian woman who declares that at their age they need to take care of themselves, and my mother agrees. She relaxes a little and also begins to appreciate rare moments of connection with her daughter. In her diary, she notes when I smile at her with sweetness, when I surprise her with biscuits and tea, and when I bring flowers to our shared room.

We live above the restaurant - a convenient location for my new job as supervisor of food preparation. Sometimes, while my body is still adjusting to the 3:00 a.m. start, I wake in the middle of the night, sit bolt upright and grab my alarm clock. This kind of behaviour worries my mother.

One morning, leaving the room in a hurry, I accidentally lock her inside. Although it warrants only a line in her diary, it causes quite a bit of hilarity among my friends. One of these friends, an American woman whose spiritual name means joy, was passing the restaurant when she heard a faint, very English voice calling out in genteel accents, "I say, I say, excuse me, hello. My daughter has locked me in." She had looked up, and there was my mother peering out through a mesh window and waving her hand. My friend would dine out on that story for weeks.

But perhaps locking my mother "in" rather than "out" was a sign that our relationship had turned a corner. My teenage rebellion had meant that I rejected her love and refused to be close, but ashram life had created an opening. Here, at least, we seemed able to connect.

Yet despite these positive changes, my mother never really feels comfortable in the ashram. When we stroll in the gardens, she finds them beautiful but recoils from the statues that seem ugly and strange. "I almost feel as if they are people if I haven't got my glasses on," she writes in her diary.

Likewise, holiday decorations and ceremonial practices around the Guru seem garish and extreme. Musical events are even worse. At the special chants, where men and women dance separately, she cannot understand why we repeat the same four dance steps for an hour or more, and the continuous chants that go on for days, and sometimes weeks, grate on her nerves. She soothes herself by walking in the gardens with headphones piping classical music clamped to her ears.

One afternoon, walking to a nearby village that is "indescribably poor and dirty with tumbledown little shops," my mother finds that she is weeping all the way down the road. There is, she observes, a "tremendous spirit about the place." She is also moved by the "beautiful orange sky with palm and banana trees etched in black," but this is offset when "frogs, bats, and lots of birds in the banyan tree make a terrible noise."

In essence, my mother is conflicted about the ashram. But by the time we travel to Bombay and confirm her flight home, she is more-or-less resigned to my continued presence here. The trip to town begins well, and my mother notes similarities between the countryside here and a landscape in Herefordshire she loves. But her tranquil mood evaporates when we reach the outskirts of Bombay. Scenes of buffaloes in the mud and goats standing on bridges have given way to human squalor.

"The mud hovels, filth and litter are indescribable," my mother observes. "There are people squatting to defecate on the sidewalk. Every time we get to lights, the beggars with mutilated stumps, armless or fingerless, are at the window with beseeching eyes. Little children say, 'Hello Mummy, chocolate, money.' I find I can hardly bear it."

The city is a mass of blaring horns and shouts, with no one paying attention to government signs instructing people not to give money to beggars or abjuring them not to make so much noise. As my mother notes, "All the lorries have HORN OK PLEASE written on the back." Our only respite comes during lunch in one of the city's expensive hotels. We enjoy the food and the immaculate service, but my mother finds the contrast with the poverty difficult to bear. On the journey home, the driver stops to discharge some errands, and an old beggar woman taps on the window. "Her face is soft with age and wrinkles, and she looks pathetic. She keeps up a perpetual soft pleading."

With her ticket confirmed, my mother has one final week at the ashram. Occasionally, she gets tearful as she contemplates my future and ruminates about young people not going to university. If she had any thoughts of persuading me to return home, she has almost abandoned them. Once, in a more desperate mood, she had tried writing a letter to my teacher. After several re-writes, she had plucked up the courage to hand it in during darshan. But when she got no obvious reply, she confessed in her diary: "I expect it to be treated with the contempt it deserved, as an attention-seeking ploy and an effort to get my way for Julia."

The diary ends abruptly. There is increased activity as she prepares for her journey home and then nothing. There is no resolution, no final word. She leaves with mixed feelings. Her heart might ache when I tell her, "You don't need to worry about me any more; my teacher will take care of me," but there are precious moments too. There was that one afternoon, for instance, when I gave her a spontaneous hug. She makes special mention of it in her diary: "Julia has not done this since she was a little girl; it was so lovely."

113

18

My mother's worst fears about cults and brainwashing having been set to rest, there was nothing to keep me from my total focus on ashram discipline and spiritual life - nothing that is except my restless mind and newly burgeoning desire.

Problems with the mind were readily addressed in evening programs or ashram books: witness the mind so you are not arbitrarily ruled by it and do the practices. If you meditate, chant, serve the Guru, and cultivate detachment you will dissolve the mind's false sense of duality and attain peace. It sounds clean and simple, although the pages of self-criticism in my journals suggest that it was not a quick or easy task.

A bigger concern was how to accept, but not act on, the promptings of my heart and my desires. Attractions in general were discouraged at the ashram, but same-sex desires seemed especially taboo. I glean this from conversations, subtle attitudes and prejudices that manifest as inner and outer circles. It is clearly best to keep one's sexuality to oneself. But in the heightened atmosphere, and on the heels of my experience with Michal, I find that my heart is tender and open. Friendships can cross easily into more intimate connections resulting in hours spent soul-searching. *Is it meaningful relationships I want or spiritual realization? With my heart open, how do I stay in the realms of exalted spiritual devotion and ignore earthly love? Or can I have both?*

There is something intensely satisfying about ashram practices when you give yourself to them. Take meditation for instance - if you get through the first layer of mind chatter, soothe your restless body, and fight off sleep you might find yourself gliding into a blissful state. It is like illumination with your eyes closed; everything seems sharper and more alive. Then there is chanting from ancient Sanskrit texts. If you can stop your mind wandering, rein in useless questions about the English translation and its relevance to modern life, and again soothe your body and stop crossing and uncrossing your legs, you can slip over the precipice into an ecstatic state. Why then isn't this enough?

Perhaps it is partly the perceived freedom that hovers around visitors to the ashram. While full-time staff members should be totally focused on the practices, devotees who live in the world are free to come and go. They stay in the ashram for a few weeks or months, soaking in the atmosphere, and then they leave, trailing worldly experiences in their wake like a whiff of exotic perfume.

Sandy, for instance, carries an aura of openness; she seems to marry her spiritual and physical life with ease. When she visits from America for several months the following year, we become immediate friends.

One still afternoon, we wander into the countryside together. My senses are heightened; my body feels like a palate from which the landscape draws colour and sensation. I hear the "choc-choc" of an axe reverberating on wood and teased by an accompaniment of tinkling goat bells. Sun hits the water on a lake and paints the reflected branches while water boatmen skitter across on long, skinny legs. As we talk, villagers pass by – men walking freely and women carrying huge stacks of wood on their heads, as if they were sticks.

For this one afternoon, spirit and body seem merged. When we walk back to the ashram at sunset, dodging the giant spider webs that leer from branches, my heart has fallen; it is coloured by love as easily as the sun paints the grasses pink and gold. *What do I do with this feeling?* Even though is has no physical expression, each time one of the monks gives a talk about focus and the dangers of wayward desires, I feel guilty. In my diary, I confess that I am "confused, afraid and unsure." My mind turns the question of love over and over like a threshing machine.

Three things save me. The first is a visit home. As soon as I get back in the environment of family, I long for the spiritual discipline of the ashram. Home feels stagnant, and I return to India with a renewed sense of commitment. When I step out of the taxi, I am flooded with a sense of homecoming. It is early morning, and the ashram is bathed in light from the rising sun. Nearby, the closed shutters of the "power laundry" mean that the two men who beat clothes against a rock have not yet woken. Cooking pots and utensils sound like timpani in the one-room apartments by the post office, and in front of me, the still, graceful body of the ashram radiates spiritual power.

The second thing that saves me is grace. Whenever I feel myself on an edge, my teacher seems to miraculously appear. One night, when she sits on a low wall in the gardens and holds an impromptu musical gathering, her presence transmutes the atmosphere; night turns into a silvery magic as if the moon and the stars had joined her entourage. All my love and longing goes into the chant, and I am determined that I will only love the Guru, the Divine Mother, from now on.

The third and final thing that saves me is Sandy's return to America. When she leaves the ashram, things go back to normal; life is simple and streamlined once again. I breathe a sigh of relief. It is so much safer to communicate through letters. With no immediate distractions, the richness of the daily schedule is fully satisfying, and in addition to the elusive goal of achieving an ego-less state, there are daily opportunities to practice detachment.

My service has shifted from chopping to making Indian snacks in the restaurant and working on the dosa grill at night. There is an art to this already perfected by my friend Rajni. With her wild curls restrained in a headband, she leans over the grill, dripping sweat, and makes dosas at lightening speed. She helps train me until I can smooth the batter on with the metal dish using just the right amount of pressure: too hard and the dosa burns, too soft and it won't roll into a crisp hollow tube. Listing between unholy pride and equally unholy thoughts of failure, dosas become the new fertile ground of my spiritual path.

Sometimes, my teacher visits the kitchen; everything sharpens when she enters as if a light has beamed in. When she walks slowly past the large mixer that we use for the dosa batter and goes over to the counter where two *sevites* are making chutney, we continue working but with senses heightened. If her fingers alight on the sides of the bowl, it is possible she will taste the contents; there is a collective holding of breath until she either smiles or makes a face and indicates the need for more lemon, salt or cilantro. On one occasion, she bites into a shiny green chili and chews without flinching, her dark eyes registering nothing. *Is that what it means to be beyond the senses?*

Five months pass quickly, and as the summer of 1984 beckons there is talk of the next American tour. A number of people have been sent out to work, and there is an air of unsettled anticipation. Silent prayers are being offered and hopes expressed, while disappointments are covered with murmurs of all things being perfect and having faith. I am one of the lucky ones; my prayers are answered, and I embark on my first American tour.

While most of the meditation centres outside India are non-residential, and devotees incorporate the practices into their existing lives, there are a few fully-fledged ashrams dotted around the world. Our final destination is the main ashram on the east coast, formed from a group of old hotels transformed into sacred space, but our first stop is in California; there, a gritty little ashram holds its own in a somewhat depressed area of a major city. We spend several months in this ashram, following the daily schedule but also holding large public programs.

Touring is a mixed blessing. It is an honour to help bring the Guru's teachings to the West, but true service means stepping beyond or rising above one's limited sense of self. And that limited self keeps tripping me up. Love of the Guru mixes with awe and shyness evoking bravery one moment and terror the next. In addition to the daunting power of her physical presence, she has exacting standards; being in tune with her means being able to read the slightest hand gesture or nod of her head. Fear makes this almost impossible.

One evening, during a public program, I am suddenly moved closer to the Guru's chair. The lights have dimmed, and we are chanting. My new responsibility is to pay attention to any signals the Guru sends regarding the lights, music or heating controls. Next to me on the wall, a dimmer switch works the lights directly overhead, and a small oscillating fan sends cool air towards the Guru's chair. I stare into the dark, watching her profile intently.

As the chant ends, we glide into meditation. I gently ease the lights down even further with a shaking hand. During meditation, my eyes stay open. *Did she just move her finger? Is she asking for an adjustment to the fan?* I stare harder, telling myself I have imagined it, while the slightly blurred outline of my teacher gives nothing away. Then she turns her head in my direction. *How am I supposed to know what that means?* I lean forward and change the setting on the fan. It whirrs a little faster. She turns her head again, more quickly. The girl in front of me leans back and switches off the fan.

My mouth feels dry. When I swallow, the back of my throat burns and my tongue clicks electronically. My left hip has gone numb, but if I change position she will notice. If I could just relax, I would be able to do this job with ease. *Breathe, Julia. Feel the oneness. Tune in. She has moved her finger again. No idea. Stay calm. If I pretend I did not see it, what will happen? Perhaps she will do it again and make it clearer. Ah, the music.*

Fortunately, the harmonium player has understood, and she is bringing us out of meditation. Up with the lights. Darshan time. Someone taps me on the shoulder. I am moved back, and another girl takes my place. Despite the burn of failure, I am relieved. Serving the Guru closely takes rigorous discipline and courage, or else one needs Rajni's brand of wide-eyed American enthusiasm; she loves the Guru without holding anything back.

Despite the pressures of tour life and talks from the Guru about rising above sense pleasure, I find time to escape into the Oakland hills with a new friend. We are not physically intimate, but we talk intensely about our lives and sometimes hold hands. For a few hours, I feel the delicious possibility of being known and a deepening sense of trust that I can reveal anything. But back in the ashram, when my teacher grasps my arm one morning and greets me in her throaty voice with a deep "aaahhhh" of pleasure and then compliments me on my chanting voice, I want nothing more than to serve her. If that means suppressing my sexuality, then it must be the best path. She is offering me so much.

119

The tour moves east, and my budding friendship and potential love are left behind. Our goodbye is quick; there is a tightness in my chest, but I won't cry. In my diary, I write: "Remember sitting on the fishing pier and the thud of waves on the wood and the sea air. Remember sitting high up on that platform in the hills holding hands and dangling legs like Tom Sawyer. Remember being still and feeling grateful for love even though it is so brief."

When at last we return to India in September, we come home with a sense of relief to be back in the beauty and stillness of the mother ashram. Although the ashram on the east coast is the twin pole of this one, with the same daily schedule, beautiful gardens, outdoor auditorium, and quiet spaces for meditation, it cannot quite mimic the extraordinary atmosphere of the Guru's home. This ashram is the central point, the still centre, and the heartbeat that sustains us when we leave each year for Europe or America. We are, perhaps, like a travelling circus: the Guru is the main attraction supported by an earnest troupe of skilled disciples ready to put her slightest commands into action.

Constant movement becomes second nature. We spend three or four months in India each year and the rest of the time touring. Jobs in kitchens, gardens, public relations, video, correspondence, and programming give me a wide smattering of skills. From time to time, I am placed in a position of directly serving the Guru, but I never get good at it. When I bring letters to her, my hands shake and my speech becomes garbled. She imitates and then waves me away. When I assist in darshan, my anxiety interferes with the simple process of introducing people and helping them ask questions. Occasionally, in a relaxed state of being, I flow with the Guru's wishes or my heart becomes so open that my fears subside. But more often, I am awkward in her presence.

To a certain extent, the qualities that make it difficult to be spontaneous around the Guru help me survive. There is something in the English nature that is geared towards endurance; we put our heads down, we adopt a stoical attitude, and we do not expect much. In comparison to some of my younger American peers, who need copious amounts of attention, I am a relatively low maintenance disciple.

Even when things are going well and I am in favour, something inside warns me not to get comfortable. I am living on the edge of grace – one moment part of a select group of girls who live above the Guru's house, and the next moment subject to a whispering campaign. Restless thoughts about leaving crop up regularly and then subside. One year, a circle of my peers plans a surprise party for my birthday. There is strawberry shortcake and meringue, and I am close to tears because of their kindness. But I know that the following year, it is just as likely that the whole day will be forgotten or ignored. Two character traits hold me separate and seem impossible to resolve: my stubborn will and my repeated tendency to fall deeply in love.

19

RAZOR'S EDGE

The Guru's main objective, in conjunction with embodying and transmitting divine love, is to destroy the ego. She will use any mean necessary, gentle or harsh, since the ego can get in the way of true surrender. This whole concept is a bit alien for those of us from the West not raised in the Guru-disciple tradition. Annihilating the ego means death of the self; it is hard to imagine what is beyond that.

For four years, I stave off restlessness and bounce back from my various affairs with a renewed desire to serve. But the question of my sexuality haunts in a seesaw of attraction and denial. Being on tour and moving between the different ashrams helps, since it is harder to form attachments, and, although I am not always aware of this, someone is usually watching; on several occasions, my role or my location changes at fortuitous moments. But while my teacher makes no overt move to suppress or control my actions, others are less restrained.

"You'll never be fully accepted if you are gay," one person says.

"You know that lifestyle does not please the Guru," another one offers.

"You need to control your senses," one of the monks declares. "How would it be if we all gave in to our desires?"

How would it be? Was it better to deny something so fundamental as my nature? Was this really the only way I could truly belong?

By January 1987, when rumours about my sexuality had begun to circulate, making for frosty relations in certain circles, it seemed as if there was only one option: give in to the subtle suggestions of the inner circle. I would marry a man I barely knew, ignore my natural sexuality, and lean in to the warm sun of approval hoping that its rays would be enough to nourish me.

Perhaps this is puzzling to anyone outside the ashram. What was the big deal some may ask? Why would you deny and betray yourself, especially in a place that purported to offer divine wisdom and insight? But in many ways, the ashram community was no different from the rest of society. It was a microcosm of the larger world, offering the same prejudices and narrow mindedness one could find anywhere at that time. While the Guru was holding out a higher vision, seeing the ends justifying the means, her disciples were often playing out their negativities or, in my case, insecurities and were more reliant on the opinions of others.

With blind and misplaced faith, I embark on my marriage plan, oblivious to its tragic and comic dimensions. My first step is to write a patently false but desperate letter to the Guru telling her I am categorically not gay. My next step is to confess that I have feelings for a man I barely know, someone suggested to me by several girls in the inner circle.

The Guru seems surprised; she asks how long it has been going on, but indicates that she has no objection. Paul, the object of my manufactured affection, is occupied fixing air conditioning units for the tour in Delhi; therefore, we are not obliged to do much actual courting. He, too, has been prodded in the direction of marriage, and I do not know his true feelings. We manage a meal in a hotel, sitting awkwardly together and wondering how we might find things in common. If various other people from the tour can see the perfection in our union, it has not yet struck us. In fact, within weeks Paul would skittishly cry off, and my matchmakers would declare him a non-starter.

This glitch in the perfect plan takes the pressure off, and I go back to falling in love with women, jumping between adoration and icy distance depending on the level of my fear. But then another character joins the stage. Rafir, known as the Guru's henchman, is a rather ruthless man who inspires more fear than respect, but he can always be counted on to get things done. When he *assures* me that he will find someone more suitable for me to marry, it appears that he has been orchestrating things all along.

In the summer of 1988, having refused the renewed attentions of the first man and dismissed another as too passive, I become aware of a third possible candidate. Secretly, I wonder if this new man is gay. He is theatrical and sensitive. Although I do not love him, I can imagine us being good friends. We date for five months and there are discussions about marriage, but he complains that I am not giving enough. When he asks how I feel about him, I am completely honest and the relationship ends.

Although I am relieved, Rafir is troubled. He seems hell bent on getting me married. He nudges me constantly and keeps asking why the relationship did not work. In February 1989, he lines up the original candidate for the third and final time. Apparently, Paul has had a change of heart after a prophetic dream.

"He wants to marry you," says Rafir, "and the Guru is very pleased."

It seems then as if my fate is sealed. If *she* is pleased, then that is all that matters. For the first time, I become officially engaged. I write home to tell my family that I am getting married, my vaguely euphoric sentences undermined slightly by a lack of basic knowledge about my future mate. But if they suspect something no one expresses it.

The tour is back in India when all this happens, and my teacher makes a point of trumpeting my engagement. She walks along a balcony of offices above the ashram courtyard and calls out to all and sundry, "Look, Gautami is getting married." People emerge from behind closed doors, offering their congratulations, and soon a line of people trails behind the Guru as if behind the Pied Piper.

It is a hollow pleasure; I am serving myself up on a silver platter, as if by will alone I could play the role of wife. Perhaps it is significant that the intended groom is once again not present during this display. He is off somewhere, tinkering with his air conditioning units, before the tour once again moves on to Delhi. Once there, we will be able to spend more time together, but our connection can only be described as amiable at best. It has been coaxed into life and fuelled by the illusion that we are submitting ourselves to divine will. In actuality, at least on my part, it is motivated by a base desire to please others and feel as if I belong.

The illusion of belonging appears as a sweet luxury, and I am determined to make the most of this new sensation. When I go into Bombay to renew my visa, I use the word *fiancé* in a conversation with an Indian woman in the waiting room and bask in her instant approval. When the tour travels to Europe and my mother visits me in Heidelberg, she too seems glad that I am doing something socially acceptable.

"We are all very pleased," she tells my teacher in the darshan line and goes home to plan an English wedding.

Pleasing others brings various temporary rewards. People treat me with renewed respect, and my job changes once again to directly serving the Guru; on my birthday that year, there is a special party, and I am showered with gifts.

But although things on the outside seem inviting, I have never felt so anxious and cut off from a sense of self. It is, bar none, the most painful experience to negate your inner knowing. What irony! I leave the stifling atmosphere of England only to tie myself in knots with this marriage of convenience. More ironies will follow.

By the time the tour returns to the east coast of America in the summer of 1989, the wedding is set for early autumn in England. Two gay friends offer to buy me a wedding dress, and I drive down to New York City for a private fitting. In their fashionable apartment, I submit to the capable but probing hands of their personal dresser. He does his best to advocate a plunging neckline with a bustier designed to make my breasts the main attraction. I have to explain that this is an ashram-inspired wedding, and he tones it down.

It is a surreal comedy of my own making, but everyone plays a part as they wait for me to either get married or own up to the deception. Perhaps it would come down to a dramatic denouement at the altar, for as the wedding draws closer, the happy couple begin to argue. A sense of desperation, of being trapped, has set in.

I write a letter to the Guru that is filled with doubts. She meets with us. Do we really want to marry or have we been told to? Why are we marrying if we don't love each other? We need to think about it. She seems to be offering a way out, and I dive for it like an osprey after salmon. I return the engagement ring within a day and call home to cancel the wedding. What a relief! But the next day, the Guru plays with us.

"How do you know you are not in love," she asks? "Perhaps you should just postpone the wedding."

The ring comes back to me, and the Guru sends us to several married couples for advice. Her choices seem extraordinary. One man describes how he ignores his wife when she rambles on, and another one makes it clear he has married his bride for money. Still, I do not get the hint. *Something must intervene to stop this. Can't anyone see I am driving with my eyes closed, back to the road, hands off the steering wheel looking desperately for the brake?*

After weeks of anxiety, numerous arguments, and the pantomime of being sent to the most unlikely quarters for advice, things come to a head when I am indecisive about attending an engagement party. Crisis hits when Rafir gives me a dressing down in public. Paul is his particular protégé, and he is furious that I have reneged on the engagement party set up by Paul's family. Since Rafir has approved this marriage, he is determined that it will take place.

He chooses to accost me at the end of a public program. My teacher is sitting in her usual chair at one end of the hall, and thousands of devotees are sitting cross–legged in front of her with men on one side and women on the other. The crowd has spilled out into the gardens, since the hall has no walls and is held up by a system of pillars. We have just enjoyed a rousing chant, and it is now time for darshan.

As beautiful music seeps out of the sound system, I stand in the darshan line thinking about my impending marriage and the cancelled engagement party. Then Rafir ambushes me. He calls my name and points to a space on the floor in front of him, close to the Guru's chair. I kneel down.

"Hey, what is the matter with you?" he asks. "Why don't you want to go to the engagement party?" His harsh middle-eastern tones seem to drill into my head. "Why are you just wasting everyone's time and money? You're being so selfish."

The Guru keeps on greeting other people in the darshan line, as if she has not heard these words.

"What is it?" he finally sneers. "Do you want a girl to marry?"

There is a stunned silence. Several people, including my teacher, look disgusted by his tactics, but no one says anything. Rafir is undaunted. He turns to a woman behind him, my supervisor, and forces her to repeat the question. She does, but her expression lets me know that she finds the whole situation appalling.

I do not answer. It is a rude exposure, and I feel as if my world is falling in on itself. Rightly or wrongly, I have believed that my teacher has not been privy to my internal struggle. I get up quickly and leave, refusing to look back and see the effect of my departure.

Back in my office, I pace up and down wondering what I should do. Thirty minutes later, I return to the darshan line and approach my teacher on the other side; I ignore Rafir, who glowers at me from across the aisle.

"I *will* go to the engagement party," I tell her desperately, rather like Cinderella. "I *will* marry him. Everything will be all right."

Again, my teacher says nothing. She half-turns towards me for a moment and smiles; then, she continues languidly greeting people with the peacock feathers. Empty and numb, I walk away. I make arrangements for a ride to my fiancé's family home in Massachusetts the following morning, and I begin packing.

But the next morning, before I can leave, the Guru summons me. She is sitting in an empty room, and I kneel nervously before her, fingering the engagement ring. She stares at me from behind sunglasses, and then in a few well-chosen words, she disabuses me of the fantasy that my marriage would somehow please her; she also exposes my underlying fears.

"I thought it was the right thing to do," I mumble weakly. "I thought I would be more accepted if I was married."

"Accepted by whom?" she asks.

"By you."

"When have I ever rejected you? When people say that, what they really mean is the people around me. The Guru has a generous heart."

She tells me that I am acting under pressure and that my constantly changing mind shows there is no imbibing, contemplation or thought.

"You're like a leaf that's blown in the wind," she declares, at the end of our conversation. "You have no inner foundation. If you want to destroy your love and your happiness, go ahead and marry him. But I never wanted it to happen."

Tears run down my face as I pull the ring off my finger.

"What do I do with this?"

"It's not mine," she answers. "Give it back to him. And stop crying; you are too emotional."

I call off the wedding and return the ring; my mother sends out cancellation notices that in some cases arrive before the original invitations. I feel a brief period of relief. It seems as if my teacher accepts me as I am; she has certainly saved me from making a terrible decision.

But underneath this feeling, there are nagging questions. *What am I really doing here? Why had my need to belong been so intense, that, for a while, I had been willing to deny myself in a misguided attempt to fit in? How can I integrate my spiritual and physical life? And am I willing to stay in the ashram if it means never having a real relationship with a woman?*

20

"I have a package for you."

The woman's eyes are a piercing blue-green. She is taller than me and athletic; she dominates the path where she has intercepted me on the way to the ashram restaurant. Since we are in India, the package sent by a mutual friend no doubt contains little luxuries that will make a lengthy stay here more palatable.

After the requisite amount of small talk, the package changes hands and we go our separate ways. Silently, I vow to avoid Mia for the rest of her three-week stay. It is exactly one year since I called off my wedding, and I am anxious to avoid trouble. But as I walk away from her, the nagging certainty of my attraction disturbs my manufactured peace.

Inevitably, we meet again. About a week later, I return to the ashram late one evening, after a dentist visit in Bombay. The restaurant is just closing, and when I take my food tray out to the pavilion, Mia is the only other person there. She greets me with enthusiasm, and we end up talking for hours; we miss the evening chant, but a posse of crows in the rafters serenade us while they search aggressively for food. We have much in common: our sexuality of course, but also love of the outdoors, a strong spiritual sense, a passion for dogs, and, perhaps most significantly, a parent who has committed suicide.

In different circumstances, our connection might have remained there – a friendship with a powerful spark of attraction – but the hint of an obstacle, a teasing unavailability, intensifies the spark.

"I'm starting a course tomorrow," Mia tells me. "I'm supposed to be in silence for the next two weeks."

We gaze at each other. The possibility of not continuing our connection, the threat of its loss, seems unbearable. Then, in a weird twist of fate, I am one of the Hatha Yoga assistants assigned to the course she is taking. Each morning and afternoon, I move among the participants adjusting their physical postures with a light touch. And each evening, Mia and I walk the grounds of the ashram without talking; silence becomes a powerful aphrodisiac. If our hands so much as brush or our shoulders touch, there is an intense electrical charge.

One of the monks gives an evening talk about the importance of being focused; he warns participants in the course not to metaphorically sully their mandatory white clothes. We take note of, but ignore, the warning, and when Mia leaves, on a full moon night in July 1990, we are romantically committed. We embrace and say our goodbye outside the ashram walls, but our intention is to stay in touch.

"Same moon," I tell her, pointing to the sky.

The days are emptier without Mia. The sudden removal of an ally creates a feeling of isolation. Plus I am restless. After the dissolution of my sham engagement the previous year, I had been sent to Europe with a small task force for public relations *seva*. We had travelled to seven different countries putting on public programs and meeting devotees, and I had loved the variety and freedom. When our group had arrived in England, I spent several days with my mother mostly talking about the past. It had been difficult to say goodbye; we had hugged in a storm of tears and the familiar feelings of love mixed with a fear of dependency.

Now, with Mia's presence in my life and the stimulus of love, it felt imperative to clear up old issues from the past and take a more active control of my life. I began to work with one of the devotees, a published writer, and in my own time sent letters to several relatives asking for their impressions and anecdotes about my father. I even took a photograph of him up in darshan, asking for the Guru's grace to heal any unresolved feelings.

My Guru's response to this internal activity was immediate and clear. She told me to join a small group of disciples engaged in vigorous Hatha Yoga training, and this activity took the edge off my restlessness and helped focus my mind. Morning, noon and night we learned the postures and honed our bodies. A special trainer was called in to push our limits - a stocky Mexican man whose résumé included training Olympians. He had us doing back flips, jumps, runs and sits-ups. Once, when I had successfully leaped one of his obstacles, he told me: "You are stronger than you think."

Care packages began arriving from Colorado with chocolate and honey, song compilations on cassette, and photographs of Mia's two miniature schnauzers set against a mountainous backdrop; life outside the ashram tasted, sounded and looked good. Thoughts of leaving continually surfaced; denial only aggravated them. In previous years, when the Guru had spoken of the difference between passions based on attachment and true love awakened from within, I had wanted to embody that wisdom. And I had paid attention when she urged us to understand that a person touching your heart is a gift of the energy not an indication you should run off with them. But my attachment to Mia proved unassailable; the sliver of space that I had forged between the Guru's will and my own grew gradually wider.

Yet after more than eight years of loving and serving the Guru, it felt heretical to imagine myself wilfully leaving. Thus it was from a place of divided longings that I eventually began my passage out, manoeuvring my way with a series of obfuscations and self-deceptions. Now, twenty years later, memory still plays tricks; I must resist the urge to clean up my tracks, cast my decisions in a clearer light, or reduce the number of desperate letters I wrote to my teacher. It is necessary to read, and re-read, letters and diary entries in order to pin down the truth.

The first letter, sent in August 1990, shortly after Iraqi troops invaded Kuwait, tells the Guru that I would like to leave the ashram in December in order to attend college. There is no mention of Mia; in fact, I propose New York as a possible place of study. This would put me close to one of the ashrams, so I could continue to serve the Guru. When she responds to my letter, she is visibly unenthusiastic; she sends me to speak with one of the trustees.

"Being near the ashram in New York would be good," he says. "That way, you can keep up your practices and avoid any temptations.

If in doubt, always ask if your actions bring you closer to the Guru."

It seems that we are all agree. Then a message comes. Rather than leave in December, it would be good to remain in India until the following spring. It seems like a reasonable suggestion. If a part of me feels anxious to leave, then the other part feels reassured that the Guru always knows best. Besides, it will give me time to research Journalism programs.

But beneath my calm exterior, I am feeling increasingly nervous. When I am around the Guru, I am filled with doubts. My second letter, sent at the end of August, does an about-face. Instead of being adamant about leaving, this letter speaks about my struggle between personal will and selfless service. What do I really want? There is no immediate answer. I spend hours talking with a close friend who is going through a similar process and has also fallen in love with a woman. When she eventually confesses everything to the Guru, she feels a huge sense of relief. She is told to leave the ashram and go out to work.

Inspired by my friend, the third letter, sent two months later, tells the Guru about my relationships with women. These relationships are challenging and confusing, I tell her, because of the ashram rules. Again, there is no direct mention of Mia. Perhaps I secretly hope that I too will be sent out to work. Instead, she sends me to a counsellor. It is surprisingly helpful. I am twenty-seven years old, and for the first time, I express sadness and anger over my father's death. Although the ashram had helped me develop in all kinds of ways, I had repressed many of the feelings that caused me to leave England in the first place. It is always love, messy and invasive, that roots out these hidden places.

But although my work with the counsellor is valuable, this kind man who skilfully takes me through imagined conversations with my father also has an agenda. He tells me to accept myself as I am, but at the same time urges me to date men. There are too many different opinions here and too many people to try and please: a lover, a teacher, a counsellor, fellow disciples, and my family who have wanted me to leave the ashram for a long time. In the face of these different and sometimes conflicting obligations, I wonder what it would it mean to please myself.

The fourth letter, sent at the end of November, thanks the Guru for sending me to the counsellor, tells her I am applying to New York colleges, and asks permission to go on a scouting tour. Permission is granted. But after a cursory tour of New York colleges, I cross the country and sneak in an unauthorized visit to Mia. Then, stepping fully over the divide, I invite her to spend Christmas with me in England.

On her home turf, Mia is spectacular. It is December when I arrive in Colorado, and the Rockies push their craggy white peaks into an endless blue sky. The streets seem filled with laughing faces, and when we drive up the Poudre Canyon for a weekend of cross-country skiing, magic unfolds. Standing on the trackless snow in Mia's spare winter clothes, ski poles lifted in wordless exaltation, I know that I belong. I am at home with the mountains, the silent pine trees, and the tall athletic woman gliding ahead of me in the snow.

In my diary, I write: "Tonight the sunset was breathtaking. I was with the dogs when suddenly I turned to look towards the mountains. The light was brilliant orange and glowing. As we walked, it changed to pink and purple, blues, violet…I felt as if the colours of my heart had escaped and were arrayed before me."

By the time I returned to the ashram at the end of December, a part of me had already left. I had even taken preliminary tests at the university down the road from Mia. Now, there was just the difficult task of informing my teacher without completely exposing my defiant will.

In darshan, I tell her that I did not like the New York colleges, and I enthuse, instead, about Colorado as if this was always part of the plan. Again, the Guru virtually ignores me; she barely glances in my direction, and the nagging feeling that things are not going well persists. Mia seems further away; the time we have spent together makes me miss our conversations even more and long for her reassuring presence. When she is with me, things make sense and anything is possible.

"I feel as if I haven't laughed or smiled in centuries," I write. "My heart misses my friend, and I cannot seem to help it."

But the part of me that loves this life of service and loves the Guru still hangs on. *How can I bear to leave? And if I must leave, how can I get the Guru's blessing? How can I be monk, lover, college student, accepted disciple and free person all at the same time?*

"The razor's edge continues," I write to Mia. "It's not like you make a decision and everything is butterflies. My instinct tells me that my teacher will have to annihilate me in some way to make it okay."

In my fifth and final letter, I tell the whole truth. Two days after I send the letter, coalition forces commence aerial bombardment of Iraqi troops, and global tensions mount. We begin a long chant for peace. Three weeks pass with no response to my letter. The conflict feels close. Each darshan is a torture; each look or word from the Guru is scrutinized.

But my letter has come too late. The Guru has grown weary of my contradictory words, my wavering plans, and my inability to own my decisions. She must have wished for more honesty than my half-truths about my choice of college or my stated desire to serve her above all else. For even as one part of me wished to stay and receive her approval, the other part had been stealthily and steadily setting up a new life. Ultimately, my instinct was right; annihilation was an inescapable part of the package.

It was a difficult leave-taking. On February 6, 1991 in an excruciating audience with the Guru and one of the monks, who holds my letter in his hand and quotes from it, she confronts my weakness. Why was I telling the Guru what to do? What had I leaned all these years? Wasn't it true that I had made my decision long ago and New York was just a front?

"Go be with what's-her-name," my Guru finally says. "There's enough sense pleasure out in the world; it doesn't need to be brought into the ashram. Go on. Pack your bags. Leave. Get out of here, and don't ever show me your face again."

"But this is my life. How can I leave?"

"Take the practices with you in your suitcase. Just don't show me your face again."

It is a curious sensation: absolute horror on the one hand, my body and mind like icebergs floating off in different directions, but a simultaneous feeling of peace. The worst has quite literally happened. The teacher whom I revere and adore is sending me away in anger; I have displeased her beyond any hope of recall.

Friends beg me to recant. The monk present at my sentencing counsels me to renounce my relationship; without asking me, he begs the Guru to extend my departure date. His request is denied. It is not even about the relationship, she says, it is my dishonesty. Since I have wanted to leave for a long time, I should just do it.

While all this unfolds, I vacillate dramatically calling Mia and telling her that the relationship is over and then calling again and saying I am not sure. But beneath the panic, there is a steadier sensation. It is my will, my reliable will, asserting itself; it is the beginning, or the remembering, of trust.

On the morning of my departure three days later, I stumble up in the darshan line and kneel at the Guru's feet. I offer a gift and then summon up some final words.

"I ask for your grace," I mumble. "I ask for your grace in the area of relationships. That seems to be my downfall."

"What did you say?" Her tone is harsh and filled with disbelief.

When I repeat my words, the Guru stares at me for a moment, and then she turns away in patent disgust. There is nothing to do but leave.

"Was that your final darshan?" an old-timer asks, when I pass her on my way out of the courtyard. Then she smiles and touches my arm. "Keep an open heart," she says.

21

LEAVING THE NEST

When I left India in February 1992, the moon was full just as it had been for Mia. I waited alone in the outer courtyard with my bags, ashamed at the manner of my exit. Most people did not even know I was leaving; those who did know either avoided me or were unsure how to treat someone so evidently out of favour. Only one person, a woman I barely knew, watched me load my bags into the taxi and waved a hand as we pulled away from the curb.

Everything slowed down; the moon seemed to own the sky. We passed the field where I used to exercise and the buildings where my mother washed bottles in iodine until the skin peeled off her hands. From the back seat of the taxi, the ashram grew smaller and smaller in the driver's mirror as my old life passed by the window and we moved inexorably on to the noises and smells of Bombay.

The day before, I had called my mother, and in a choked voice told her I was coming home.

"What is it darling? What's the matter? What's happened?" She had asked in quick motherly bursts.

"It's all right," I had tried to reassure her. "I'll tell you when I get home."

Home: the thought is more comforting than Mia's questions or her outrage. At the Bombay airport, several Europeans returning from a visit to the ashram join my flight. Kind, and ignorant of my dilemma, they soften the journey to Paris which was the closest destination I could get at such short notice. But Europe is in the grip of a cold snap, and my connecting flight is delayed for several hours. My mother reports that there is snow on the ground.

"Michael will come and fetch you from the airport," she says, over the phone.

"No, no. I don't want to see anyone else." My voice flays like old rope. "I'll take a taxi. Please let me take a taxi."

The plane circles and lands like a hungry vulture, and in the landing corridor the cold air bites my skin. A black taxicab, more at home in London than the suburbs, carries me along the icy roadways at a sedate pace. By the time we reach the outskirts of Leatherhead, it feels as if we have trekked for days. As the taxi turns into the driveway, rolling past the barren rose-beds towards the house with its square solid frame, I am aware that this is my last journey home. Hillside is going to be sold, and the house that holds my memories will pass into someone else's hands.

My mother hears the taxi, and she rushes from the house, calling my name with a blend of relief and joy that I am home. She hugs me tightly, as if to make certain that I am whole. We carry my bags inside and close the door. Michael and Caroline arrive a short while later, and we dig out the old toboggan, smother ourselves in coats and scarves, and trudge to a field thick with snow and bright with flying dots of colour. We slide into crusted tracks and race down the hill in a rush of cold air and the grate of rusty runners.

The day passes like a half-waking dream, sheltered by the tactful voices of family who act as if my return was planned. But once they leave, once my mother and I possess the house again, bits of my story come out like reluctant shadows. Over the next few weeks, we take long walks and ruminate about spiritual life. My mother thinks the ashram is too confining. Why shouldn't you make your own decisions? And what's wrong with loving women if that is how you are made? Spirituality, she insists, is internal and not dependent on the outer form of the teacher or any particular ritual.

Since I resent any direct criticism of my teacher, my mother does her best to suppress her natural indignation. There is so much that needs sorting out, but no one can helpfully pronounce on what has happened; this has to be my story. My exit had been hastened, harshly perhaps, but I was the source of the upheaval. I had substituted suppression and denial for true surrender, and now I must live out the consequences.

It seemed, as my mother and I walked across the downs on ground that had been left sodden with the passing of snow, that nothing in my life could ever be the same again. With my teacher's dismissal of me, a rejection that now sat on top of my father's absence like a heavy burden, all external props had been stripped away. For the first time, I would have to consistently rely on my own definitions of value and truth.

But mother's love comes with anxiety - a thick sticky substance born in mother's milk. It seeps, it spreads, and it mixes in your system so that anxious minds work in unison like a generator kicking in. After the first flush of relief, when my mother was concerned with my immediate welfare, she began to question my decisions. When I shared plans for studying in Colorado and living with Mia, she baulked at what she considered my lover's forceful personality.

When Mia had visited the previous Christmas, her lively confidence had left a strong impression; exuberance that would have been appreciated in America apparently felt overwhelming in the confines of my mother's small cottage. At the time, only my sister-in-law had noticed we were lovers; the rest of the family just referred to Mia as my "American friend." But now that Mia was my official lover, my mother misguidedly wondered if I had been pressured into being gay. It was the first time that I regretted having kept her in ignorance of my sexual history.

"What will your life be like?" she wonders. "Why do you always do things the hard way?"

Temporarily, we dismiss anxieties and join two of my mother's friends on a ski trip to France. It is my first time skiing, and the focus needed to keep me upright is the perfect remedy for my post-ashram malaise. Out on the slopes, there is nothing more important than finding the edge on my skis, learning to snowplough, practising turns and always keeping a measurable distance from the edge of any precipice.

We stay in a chalet, and I sleep in a tiny bed tucked in the wall and reached by way of a small ladder. Each day is spent on the slopes, and each evening we return to the chalet and one of us cooks. All three of the women are mothers, and since mother's day falls in the middle of our trip, I surprise them by going to the local boulangerie and returning home with pastries and apple tart. Attentions to the body such as exercise, good food and wine induce a slow thaw.

❧

By the time I leave for Colorado in May, I am stronger than when I first left the ashram, but some of the anxieties come with me. It is hard to tear myself away from my mother's love, and now I am a spiritual outcast, a lesbian, and a non-resident alien in the strangely apt language of my new home. Mia does her best to welcome me to Colorado, but she cannot package things with the same innocence and purity as before.

Adjusting to life outside the ashram proves difficult. For weeks, I test Mia's patience by crying at the drop of a hat and refusing to unpack all of my things. Sadness lies leaden between us, and my shy, optimistic illusions about love and Guru's grace seem shattered beyond immediate repair. I write in my journal about missing Mum with a strange intensity, as if her life should not be going on without me. I wonder if I will ever feel self-worth again.

I cast around for a new sense of meaning: make my life a work of art; appreciate each moment; ease out from under the burden of other people's expectations; love myself. Mia draws me a map of the town and surrounding areas, and I begin to explore.

But the air feels strange, as if an element is missing, and mundane tasks are absent of ritual and stripped of meaning. The simplest things feel overwhelming. When I fuel my lover's car, for instance, I leave the pump handle down and gasoline spills over my hand and on the ground. Grocery stores, a symbol of nurture, are huge warehouses filled with plastic and fluorescent lights. The home that I am sharing with Mia, a townhouse quite close to the university, expresses her tastes rather than mine. Still, I send my mother cheerful updates, focusing more on the freedom of our shared home than Mia's need

142

for things to match – furniture, clothes, picture frames, cars. I don't tell her that it is hard to know where my sense of taste begins or ends.

In June, Mia takes me to a cabin in the mountains for my birthday. She cooks pasta, boiling it in a big pot on an open fire, and serves it with a tomato sauce in blue-flecked aluminium bowls; we eat at a picnic table close to a rushing river. Mia moves confidently, at home in the outdoors. When she hands me a bulky package wrapped in newspaper, I discover a hikers' backpack – purple and teal – with a matching fleece top, cap and bandana. There is so much that is good in this new life.

In July, we go home to England for a visit. I have a scheduled surgery – a breast reduction that I have wanted for some time – and Mia has come to offer support. But she and my mother compete for my attention. It is bad enough that the doctor who performs the surgery ignores my desired breast size and declares that I need a "good British handful"; it is worse that the two people I love most are subtly fighting. Before and after the operation, they vie for the role of caretaker; Mia wins. She takes good care of me, but the funny stories filtering back about their cohabitation and their miscommunication, despite a common language, makes me feel as if two sides of me are warring.

Only nature offers uncomplicated beauty. When we return to Colorado, I take solace in the mountains that cut a jagged line on the western horizon and spend hours walking the dry, rocky paths among the pine. One morning, when I am walking in the foothills, a herd of deer thunders through a shallow reservoir; the sight of their majestic bodies streaming through the water and up the bank on the other side seems a portent of strength and freedom.

Mia's dogs accompany me on these adventures, and when they have puppies, it is inevitable that the runt of the litter should fall, quite literally, into my hands. Mia is away when they are born. The mother comes scrabbling at my feet, and when I follow her back to the large cardboard freezer box set up as a maternity ward, the puppies come quickly. I catch and dry each one and then set them close to their mother, nestled against a hot-water bottle we have christened Tired Tiger.

When the runt comes, somewhere in the middle of the litter, she stands out. Her head is too large for her body, and her tiny ribs are like delicate metal staves. She is too weak to suckle, but she accepts milk from a dropper with her too-large head held between my fingers then flopped on her small heaving chest. I christen her Idgie, and when prospective buyers come, we hide together until they leave. Eventually, Mia accepts that we are a two-person, three-dog household, and I don't feel so alone.

22

It is university life that provides the cocoon for my development. Striding the campus with my backpack of books and the goal of an undergraduate degree in Journalism with a minor in English, I feel a sense of purpose developing. And my earnest application, noticeable among a gaggle of eighteen year-olds, endears me to my teachers. It helps that the head of the English Department is a lesbian who commands respect. Pattie is erudite, wise, and incredibly kind. She is a respected academic, a personable individual, and someone who naturally helps to counter ignorance and prejudice through her ethical life and her sustained partnership with a woman.

When I first encounter her, she is a guest speaker in a women's studies class I am taking. She is small in stature with a serene face and hair so fair and fine it is almost white; she wears her hair cut short, in a simple style, and her clothes are similarly functional and plain. What I notice most strongly is her calm attention – the way she listens to students and then answers them thoughtfully, always remembering their names. She has a way of explaining things that slips below the obvious and takes you deeper into a subject, although it is hard to say how you got there.

I sign up for one of her literature classes, intrigued by the self-reflective creative writing component. Our first assignment is to write something that serves as an autobiographical introduction to the class. In an unusual gesture, designed to put us on an almost-equal footing, Pattie includes herself in this assignment and writes about a recent Thanksgiving dinner. The plan is to read our pieces aloud and then put them in a binder that will serve as one of the texts for the class.

I labour at my writing and produce something honest and revealing that includes a revelation about my sexuality. It is unfamiliar ground for me, and after the repression of the ashram, I am eager to push the limits of this new identity. There is a hint of defensive challenge as I read; I want to be accepted, but it has to be on my terms.

When Pattie reads her peice, I enjoy the subtle depictions of her family's ranch in Montana, the background of life working the land, the images of an extended family gathered to appreciate good home cooking. But there are no clear references to her partner, just vague hints that she is there with someone; it is all so understated. Since I had imagined, and possibly invented, an unspoken solidarity between us, I now feel sold out. Unreasonably, I had expected her to expose her sexuality in the same way that I had exposed mine.

At a faculty party several days later, I confront her. Why had she been so coy in her writing? Why hadn't she identified her partner? Her reasonable answer, that she was sensitive to her role as teacher and did not feel it was necessary to make this issue front and centre, does little to mollify me. But before I can say more, Pattie entirely captures my allegiance.

"It occurs to me that you are angry," she says. "Why don't we meet for tea or coffee, and we can talk about this? Come to my office and we will set a time."

In that simple acknowledgment, especially one that named my anger but did not reject it, I felt that I had encountered a genuine teacher. We did meet, more than once, and she listened patiently to my experiences and shared some of her own. She also guided and helped nurture my genuine passion for literature and my budding awareness of feminist issues. She would be a good friend to have during the turbulent years ahead when the state of Colorado would go through an ugly political process debating whether gay people could be denied civil rights. For months, our town of just over a hundred thousand would be bitterly divided, and allegiances and prejudices would fight for space on public and private billboards.

For now though, the only divisions were the ones that were starting to appear at home. On the surface, things were progressing

146

well. We had moved out of Mia's townhouse and bought a home together, and I was gainfully employed as a feature-writing intern at a local newspaper where my biggest concerns were melding my English sensibilities to write convincingly about 4-H clubs. For her part, Mia was in the midst of a career change, and she was excited about the possibilities ahead. But beneath this positive exterior, tensions existed and from time to time they would erupt.

My mother came to visit, and we went camping in the Maroon Bells. The scenery was glorious; the wildflowers were showing in exuberant bursts of colour, and the distant peaks were delicately snow-covered. My mother had even reluctantly put on shorts and boots, making her seem younger than her years, and although she struggled with the altitude, she was doing her best. But at night, she was miserable, sleeping on the floor of the tent between the two of us on her too-thin mat and her woeful sleeping bag. Somehow, we were unable to laugh this off, and a strange atmosphere developed. Again, it felt as if I was being pulled between two differently charged poles.

When it comes, Mia's change of career is dramatic. She goes from special education teacher to motivational speaker in one large bound. Suits replace her formerly relaxed clothing, and she begins to spend days on the road learning her craft with a public company before she goes out on her own. When she returns from these trips, she needs quiet and solitude. I, on the other hand, am craving conversation and demonstrations of love. The more Mia recedes, the more urgent my demands. My unmet needs, legacy of that early loss, manifest in desperate efforts to change her behaviour in order to make myself feel good.

Mia is blossoming, and I am suddenly feeling like the shadow to her sun, the foil to her main act, always pushing to find my own patch of ground. Threatened by a more dominant personality, I express myself in small, futile acts. When Mia had suggested buying one of the early computers, for instance, I had ignored her advice and continued to pound out my essays on a portable electric typewriter for several arduous semesters.

Arguments become more common. Our relationship, marked from the beginning by my difficult exit from the ashram, cannot withstand the pressure of all the necessary change. It is, after all, my first real relationship. I am rough material - a fledgling in this new chapter of my life – and love has turned out to be something other than the romantic fantasy I had imagined.

My Guru had been right; attachment gives rise to jealousy and anger, and the ease of letter writing does not prepare you for living with someone on a daily basis. Counselling helps, but finding a suitable practitioner takes time. One man offers insights about the ashram but has a limited view of relationships. A female practitioner explains relationship patterns, but she focuses too heavily on speech tags; a pantomime with Mia ensues where we both take pains to put "I feel" statements at the beginning of our accusations.

"Now that you have Idgie," Mia declares one day, on the heels of an argument, "you will probably feel free to leave."

But when the inevitable ending comes, approximately three years after we had met, *both* of us are longing to leave the relationship. I move into the loft room, we put our house on the market, and Mia begins to systematically get rid of things associated with our former life. Secretly, I recover letters and favourite mugs from the trash. It is an ugly unravelling – privacies violated, promises broken, and my lover and then me in new relationships before either of us have completed the disappointments of this one.

A new counsellor helps. Kathy is in her sixties – tough yet wise. She validates my sexuality and understands the subtle layers of conflict that have dogged me from my earliest days. Together, we explore enmeshment with my mother, the push-pull stimulated by the circumstances of my father's death, and various underlying emotional patterns. I gauge the power of my sessions by the number of tissues I use. It is a slow, steady process of self-discovery bolstered by moving out of the home I shared with Mia and into one of my own.

With independence comes a new sense of my strength and abilities. I stay on for a Masters Degree in English, paid for with a teaching assistantship, and Pattie becomes my mentor. We co-teach a class, and I admire her particular skill of marrying soulful depth with literary insight. She has a life that I could imagine for myself.

My newfound confidence is tested when the battle over Amendment 2 comes to town. The bill seeks to deny gay people minority status and could potentially pave the way for public and private discrimination. When I walk down a street, I can guess which houses might welcome me by displays on the front lawns and the presence or absence of an American flag flying righteously in the breeze.

Although the discriminatory bill passes, it is immediately challenged in the court of appeals. Many in the community publicly oppose the hate campaigns conducted in the name of family values. And when a young gay man, Matthew Shephard, is brutally murdered just across the border in Wyoming, the issue gains a personal face and national attention. Matthew dies in our local hospital in October 1998, and there are public discussions, candlelight vigils, and moving speeches by the boy's mother who becomes a powerful campaigner for gay rights.

My relationship to all this is charged and personal. I do not campaign on the streets of Colorado; I process and ruminate, write and reflect. *What does it mean to be human? Why would love cause such hate?* In a letter home, I try to explain my feelings about Matthew Shephard's death and why it feels so personal. My mother is sympathetic; Michael is silent; Richard, who has already expressed his disbelief about my sexuality, declares that there are greater tragedies and that one death does not amount to much. Besides, he speculates, the young man probably brought it on himself.

As a result of his words, I almost boycott my brother's wedding on an Indonesian Island. But my wise counsellor advises me to attend and suggests that I stop trying to get Richard to accept my lifestyle.

"Live your own life," she tells me. "Love your family, and don't try to control others."

It is good advice that will take years to live into. There are more relationships to follow like a string of fairy lights stretching across Colorado to Wisconsin where I eventually move for graduate school. Each relationship begins with promise, each is filled with sublime moments and betrayals, and each becomes part of a much larger project that maps my unconscious. As I ride the tracks laid down in childhood, I systematically look outside myself for approval or chase unavailable loves in an effort to feel whole. But with each relationship, with each new understanding, a piece of myself is uncovered and returns home.

23

TRANSITIONS

By the time I leave Colorado in the summer of 1999, I have two degrees, a legacy of wonderful but messy relationships, a tidy profit from the sale of my house, a vanload of furniture in Mia's preferred heavy oak style and two miniature schnauzers. Idgie, who was used to living with other dogs, had acted up once we were alone. Although she loved our house on the edge of a park that filled seasonally with goose droppings, she began overturning waste paper bins, shredding tissues, and sneaking into the cupboard under the sink to feast on kitchen remains. When Little Bit had appeared in a pet shop one day, clearly another runt, I had ignored my sensibilities and brought her home.

This new arrival was short, stocky and looked, according to one friend, like a javelina. For several months, she conducted a charm campaign by dropping passively to the floor, rolling over, or placing one shy inviting paw on Idgie's proud head. By the time they eventually became friends, Idgie had firmly established her role at the top of the food chain beyond any shadow of doubt.

When the three of us left Colorado, it was on a typically warm day in June. The sky was clear, the sun was bright, and as we headed down to Denver the mountains shimmered beside us in a slightly polluted haze. My Nissan Pathfinder was already quite full; Idgie and Little Bit had been forced to nest among bags, blankets, dog beds and boxes of various kinds. Despite this, we were on our way to collect more luggage, another passenger, and two extra dogs.

Some years after our separation, when hurts were forgotten and feelings soothed, Mia and I had resumed our friendship. Now, by some strange quirk of fate, she was re-locating at the same time as I was. Indiana, her destination, was more or less on the way to Wisconsin, and we had agreed to ride together. It meant a later start, but it would be nice to have someone to share the driving.

As I look back now, the journey seems to reflect aspects of myself that were unconscious and had yet to heal. Despite all the inner work I had done, I was sometimes slow to recognize my feelings and, in the face of stronger personalities, prone to giving myself away. So while the move to Madison, Wisconsin appeared purposeful and clear - graduate school lined up, a home ready to purchase, and all the indications of a fresh new start - there were a few hidden spots and ragged edges. I had moved on a little recklessly, severing one or two friendships that no longer worked and starting an affair just before I left town. Moving away from Colorado and upending my life had apparently stirred hidden anxieties, the old places of childhood, and I had not been fully conscious of my underlying needs.

When my laden car arrives in Denver, Mia is still cleaning the house that she and her now ex-girlfriend have just put on the market. Her bags, piled in the hallway, are far more numerous than I had expected, and it is immediately clear that I will need to ship some of my larger items including my computer.

"I'm just going to find a shipping place," I tell her, "do you need anything?"

"How about a smoothie?" she replies.

Neither of us has eaten lunch, and a bit of nourishment might ease the gathering tension about our late start. I drive off, leaving Mia to her pressing domestic duties. When I return an hour later, having shipped my computer in a box crammed with various bits of clothing and enough packing material to ensure its safe passage, I have a somewhat emptier car and two large to-go cups.

As I walk across the threshold, my foot catches on something; two blackcurrant smoothies sail slowly, impossibly, into the air and spill all over the white pile carpet.

"Oh my god. The house is being shown tomorrow," Mia shrieks.

"We can clean it."

"How? It's Saturday. None of the carpet cleaning places will be open. What are we going to do?"

We call everyone imaginable: carpet companies, family members, and friends. Everyone offers different advice. We finally get the stains up using a warm iron and a brown paper bag; it is quite miraculous. But we are now way behind schedule, and I have a house closing in less than forty-eight hours. With this deadline hanging over our heads, we pull away from the kerb with the car stuffed to the gills, bags on the roof, and four miniature schnauzers almost ceiling-high.

"Lets stop and get something proper to eat," I say, responsibly.

"No, we really need to push on," Mia insists. "We're going to have to drive through the night as it is."

"But I need to eat something. I don't do well on an empty stomach."

"Okay, we'll stop on the outskirts of town," she promises.

But we don't stop. We keep driving all the way to Nebraska where we fuel up and make-do with thin slices of dried-out pizza. The burdened car moves on relentlessly. Mia seems able to go without sleep. I try to nap, head lolling against the cold window, but at midnight, when my driving shift is supposed to start, I still feel tired. Mia teases me and recalls past incidents of slow night driving, but she stays at the wheel.

As we roll out of Iowa and tip into Indiana early the next morning, I am anxious to do my part. Although my head feels disconnected from my body, I take the wheel and drive on in the near dark of early morning while Mia sleeps. There is a curious peace; I am the only one awake in the car, and yet there is the comfort of tiny dog snores and Mia's softened face.

My awareness drifts for just a moment. We are on the outskirts of a town called Galesburg in Indiana. There are road works, and the edge of the highway is steeper than usual. When I drift, head nodding forward into sleep, the front tyre catches the high lip of the kerb. The noise and pull of the tyres startle me instantly awake. I jerk the steering wheel back. For a moment, we hang in the balance, top-heavy and teetering like an old-fashioned livery coach, and then the car begins to fishtail. Time slows; we swish and flail from side-to-side slowly gathering momentum. Mia wakes and lifts her head.

"What's happening?" she asks.

I reach out and clasp her hand, witnessing the moment clearly and calmly.

"Don't worry," I tell her, speaking almost word for word the quote from my Guru that sits on the dashboard of my car. "Don't worry. Everything will be all right."

Mia loses consciousness when her side of the car hits the road and drags, filling her upper arm with tar and ripping the fingernails off one hand. I stay awake through the impossibly slow roll, feeling trapped and helpless at the centre of the vortex. We land right side up, and the car shudders to a stop partway down a bank, blocked by some kind of railing or pipe.

People arrive from nowhere. Someone has found two of the dogs out on the road and picked them up. A man prevents me from climbing out of the window. Someone else calls the emergency service. The hours pass. We are cut from the car and transported on stretchers. Three of the dogs are taken to an animal hospital for safekeeping, but one is still missing. Later, the fourth dog is found trapped at the back of the vehicle, unharmed like the others.

Mia requires stitches and must be kept overnight in hospital; despite her pain, she jokes from the next-door room that if she has to have an anal probe then I should have one too. But I am fine, free to roam in hospital scrubs while I wait to the garage where the car has been towed. It is a wreck of mangled metal. I sort through bags, audiotapes, dog beds and anything that has survived the crash. My miniature Piglet is merely tar-stained, but a statue of Buddha has been severed in half. Everything is covered in broken glass; my old life has quite literally been shattered.

That night, in a hotel room with four terrified yet physically sound dogs and a pile of tarnished possessions, I call friends just to hear them speak. At five in the morning, the woman who has driven through the night in her small red Honda to rescue me walks quietly through the door. We leave Mia in the tender hands of her new lover, pack the Honda and drive more than three hundred miles to Madison with me at the wheel. Although I flinch at each sound, refuse to change lanes, and find it difficult to judge the distance between car and kerb, we make it to the house closing only ten minutes late.

It is a difficult beginning, made worse when the moving van is delayed and we are forced us to sleep on an air mattress between bare walls; confidence is at low ebb. The house itself is charming, a two-story Cape Cod in a quiet street on the east side of town, but without my familiar things it seems vacant. When my friend leaves at the end of a week, a sense of loneliness permeates my days.

For several more weeks, I keep responding to the crash; the sound of car brakes sends adrenalin shooting through my veins and anger lurks below the surface of my skin. It takes time and the simplicity of daily presence before my body slowly releases the trauma and trusts life once again. My breathing slows and deepens; furniture settles in the new home; the dogs acclimatize to their narrow garden; and the town and university take shape before my eyes. Eventually, the accident and my Colorado life feel like a distant memory.

It is the new millennium, and I have been re-made. The world has not come to an end as expected. Those who have stockpiled emergency supplies, anticipating months in basements eating canned food and drinking bottled water, can now consume these goods at leisure. For my own part, I am grateful for a new beginning and eager to do well in graduate school.

This proves harder than I had anticipated. The PhD program seems designed to foster feelings of inadequacy. Theory classes are opaque, the teaching load is considerable, and literature seminars require ever more complex social, cultural and historical interpretations. There is no softer side; all the work that I have done on my personal self, unearthing and integrating emotions, seems unvalued and irrelevant in a place that privileges rigorous intellectual debate.

For months, I fling myself against the structures of academia and waste energy opposing the very system I had signed up for. I speak up in classes, resist competitive pressures, demand accessible language and try to find acceptable ways to write about emotion in literature. It colours my experience of daily life, and I do not immediately appreciate the relaxed atmosphere of the town, its emphasis on outdoor activity, and its beautiful setting around two large lakes; I question whether I belong.

"It's not the place that's the issue," a friend tells me. "Don't give up on these people. You are just cut off from your heart and your spirituality."

After seven years absence, I visit the Guru in upstate New York. The ashram feels sweetly familiar, and the chants and meditations anchor me once again in my personal practice. If some old friends are distant, others are welcoming, and I am happily ignorant of all behind-the-scenes drama. I am there purely for my spiritual health.

In the darshan line, emotions surge through me as if my heart is playing different chords: love for the Guru, poignancy over my exit, flashes of fear, and finally gratitude. I can feel a foundation of self-trust that would not have been possible seven years before.

The Guru is radiant, and when I bow low, tears drying on my cheeks like sea spray, I do not immediately get up. I stay there, kneeling in front of her with nothing left to hide.

"It is so good to see you again," I tell her.

She turns at last, swats me with her feathers and smiles.

"Aaaah, you are looking well," she says.

It is enough. It is a kind of closure. As I walk away, the Guru sends a young girl after me bearing a soft grey cushion embossed with a koala bear. She hands me the cushion, and, as I hug it to my chest, I have a clear and peaceful understanding that the ashram is no longer my place. There had been a time for close contact with my teacher, and there had been a long and painful separation, but now all that was over. The visit would allow me to move forward without regret. While the experience of the ashram would remain as a spiritual grounding, there would now be room for other spiritual circles, other friends, and other ways to turn within.

Gradually, my life in Madison finds its balance. If graduate school remains a challenge, it is counteracted by the richness of my personal and home life. My mother visits and we make a garden;

I dig out the beds, while she painstakingly shakes the loose earth from each clump of grass. Together, we plant roses, rhododendrons, peonies, sedum, lavender and wild geranium. Two years later, when I leave this house and move in with a girlfriend called Patti, most of the plants come with me. And when the dryness of academic life feels too much, I cry and rail in Patti's arms, sinking into the comfort of her more tactile presence.

24

When the plane touches down in the massive Denver airport in July 2008, Colorado is still under snow. The high mountains are impassable without picks and crampons, so my friend Kim and I opt for the warmer and slightly lower peaks of New Mexico. We choose a route in the Pecos wilderness and drive down in her truck loaded with packs, food, and a gangly dog called Zeek.

After my long visit home to England, six weeks in America is a welcome break. At the airport, the lines, the security questions, removing my shoes all felt like foreplay to the ultimate pleasure of being back in the United States. As I sat on a bench waiting to board the plane, I had scanned the faces and bodies of my fellow passengers: woman in tivas and khaki pants, probably American; guy in baseball cap also American; young boy asking his sister if she wants a Pepsi, American despite his English looking face. I had immediately felt at home amongst them.

The backpacking trip would also be a familiar pleasure - my last trip for a while, unless I was willing to brave the unpredictable English weather. Soon, I would gather up my possessions in Madison, re-unite with Little Bit, and start the real journey home by land and sea. These wide vistas, this untrammelled earth, would be replaced by boxed-in towns and muted, pretty farmland.

We stop for the night in a campground, sleeping in the truck with Zeek stretched out between us so we are ready for an early start. When daylight comes, we stretch our cramped bodies, brush teeth, swallow tea and oatmeal, and ease the truck out past the straggling line of tents and campers before most people are stirring. Several hours later, we reach the trailhead, driving up among aspen and pine, and nudge the truck into a line of already parked vehicles. Behind us, horse riders have set up a base camp with trailers and fenced off paddocks, and the air is rich with smells of coffee, breakfast, and manure.

We make the last amendments to our clothing, leave unnecessary food in the truck, and fill our water containers. Adjusting to the unaccustomed weight of our packs, we head off in a steady climb up a series of switchbacks. The air is thinner, forcing a slower pace, but the path is springy with pine needles and my hiking pole gives me an edge. The sounds of cars recede, voices grow fainter, and our senses tune to the more subtle language of the outdoors. A light breeze stirs the pine needles; a squirrel or chipmunk sends a pinecone rattling down among branches; a tree root stretches across the path in search of moisture.

When we break out into a meadow, we stop for lunch with a stunning view out over the mountains. Below us, a river forges its way through a lush valley scattered with homes. A horseman passes, angling his steed up the mountain with easy hands. He tells us to keep an eye out for wild cattle and then disappears over the crest of a hill. We wait until he is far ahead of us then load up our packs and journey on.

We will hike each morning, trying to stay ahead of the afternoon rain showers heralded by black lowering clouds and a chilling wind. On the first day, rain hits us in an open area. We pull on rain gear, cover our packs as best we can, and move quickly towards a distant stand of trees. We dry out, arguing a little about staying put versus pushing on. Kim eyes the sky uneasily, calculates the distance to our first camping spot and insists we keep going. The rain drives towards us, and we mistake animal tracks for the path. We argue again when the tracks run out on a hillside forcing us to backtrack, re-read the map, and focus our attention more precisely. These tensions and small miscalculations are all part of the first day; we must remember patience, sensitivity, and a deeper respect for our environment.

When we break for camp, it is late afternoon; we are damp and a little tired. We take to our allotted tasks quietly: put up the tent, boil water, re-fill the camelbacks, feed Zeek and make crude drying lines from our extendable hiking poles. Dinner on the first night is simple: hot water into instant food packets followed by mugs of herbal tea. When we spread the map on our knees and mark out the route for the next day's hike, we agree on an earlier start.

But when morning comes, and the sun warms our bodies, we are reluctant to hurry. We have spent the night with damp clothes at the bottom of our sleeping bags, and it is tempting to lay them out on the sun-kissed rocks. Hot tea and cereal taste good, better when eaten leisurely, and the morning rituals feel soothing. As we roll up sleeping bags and mats, shake out the tent, discuss water supplies, and check and re-check our packs, we slide into a natural coalescence.

Our unity is tested on day three, when my pace lags and altitude sickness sends me diving into the bushes at regular intervals. Kim and Zeek hike ahead of me and slowly the distance between us lengthens. On a high ridge, marked at intervals by piles of stones and the collected dry bones of animals, they fall completely out of sight. Disoriented and without a map, I scream into the wind, my voice echoing in the mountains; Kim waits for me at the next marker. My body feels wracked, but we head on, aiming for a lake that seems further than the mile markers suggest. Our water supplies are dwindling, and my lips feel like cracked earth. But one more turn, a narrower track, a slight rise and then we climb down into a bowl; the lake is before us.

It is double exposure: the water has pulled the clouds, mountains and trees into its still depths. Peaks rise to the sky but also go down to the centre of the earth. We take off our packs and open our senses to the beauty that absorbs whatever tiredness or frustrations we thought we had. On one side of the lake, streams tumble down the hillside amid purple and red wildflowers and the occasional flash of dragonfly wings. On the other side, a waterfall purrs and crashes in the waning afternoon sun.

I trade hiking boots for tivas, pull warm fleece pants over my shorts and cover my sun-touched arms with a long-sleeved shirt. Free of the pack, my body feels weightless. Below me, a pocket of land juts into the lake, and the grasses are matted down as if some animal has slept there. When I close my eyes, sitting near the water

161

in complete surrender, I sense my mother's presence. Silently, I offer a prayer for her nourishment; several days later, I will learn that she had not been well.

That night, after a hot dinner of split-pea soup and potatoes, the moon rises and enters through the mesh of our tent. We read for a while in twin pools of light, and then, like Zeek, curl up with a deep and contented sigh.

The morning comes with clear skies and just enough sun to warm us when we step outside the tent in long underwear and woollen hats. We lay out our clothes and sleeping bags and put hot water on to boil.

"Can't we stay here one more night?" I ask. "My body is only just beginning to feel normal again."

"We should keep moving. The lake is beautiful, but there might be even greater views ahead."

Kim might be right; besides, we have divided our days into manageable eight or nine-mile hikes. Reluctantly, we re-pack, check the map again, and pump fresh supplies of water from the stream. With one last look at the mirror lake, we follow the path out and drop down through woods. When the land evens out into a rocky trail, packed on one side with snow, we press on and cross a long mountain ridge stalked by wind and littered with dry pieces of wood. Some pieces are curled and twisted in dancing patterns, and one piece looks like a woman carrying a child in her womb. This comes with me along with a few precious stones.

After the long traverse under the threat of dark clouds and distant lightning, the path slopes down again into more woods. We hear voices. Quite suddenly, we are in a forest of tents and hikers. They have come from the opposite direction, carrying the noises of civilization, and the contrast to our previous solitude is unbearable. We agree to keep walking out instead of camping, almost twice the distance we had originally planned for that day.

My pack is heavy now. It slips down over my hips, numbing them, and bumps the size of golf balls develop along my collarbones. I synch the pack tighter, hoist it up, and follow Kim in a steady climb down. We move at a brisk pace through woods damaged by heavy storms. Great trees have been ripped out of the ground and their roots exposed, as if an angry giant has stomped through. When I straddle one of the fallen trees, my feet do not reach the ground; it feels as if I am touching living flesh. But it is a graveyard, and we walk on in sombre mood.

The afternoon is fading when we finally reach the truck. My legs feel like timber; even Zeek slumps down with head between paws. But once the packs are eased off, once hot feet escape from boots, a slow satisfaction spreads through our bodies. We dangle our legs off the flatbed of the truck and re-live the hike.

It is tempting to stay there, luxuriating in the memory and gift of effort, but the thought of a real meal draws us down the mountain while it is still light. As we follow the winding road and finally slip onto the highway, my body adjusts to the cars, mechanical noises and artificial lights. I am grateful that we are still in open land; at least the air outside the truck still smells of sage and the wind ruffles my matted hair.

We drive first to Santa Fe, a place I had visited years before on one of the ashram tours. Back then, we had arrived in winter, and the ground had been covered in snow. Some of us made a snowman and invited the Guru to visit our A-frame lodgings that smelled strongly of smoke. She had admired the snowman and then watched us throw snowballs at each another in a mock fight. The rest of that visit to Santa Fe had not been as pleasurable. I had performed poorly in my role as darshan girl, and when I ran down the centre aisle one evening to deliver a wand of peacock feathers that had arrived late, it had been the final straw. My behaviour did not embody the serene, discipline and discreet focus that the Guru was looking for. But that was how we learned. The Guru's displeasure and her high standards were put to good ends; most of the skills that have sustained me in life were learned there in the ashram.

Kim and I make only a brief overnight stay in Santa Fe. We tour several art galleries, eat a fantastic breakfast, and then drive seventy miles north and slightly east to Taos, a town in the north-central region of New Mexico. The previous year, after three months in Arizona unsuccessfully applying for a job and trespassing on the

163

hospitality of a friend, I had stopped for the night in Taos en route to Colorado. When my friend, Angi, had unexpectedly needed a dog sitter, I had remained there for more than a month.

Taos had been a place of refuge. Three long months in Arizona after graduation had left me dry, and the hardest part of it had been losing my dog, Idgie. She had loved the warm climate, but, at fifteen, her body had shrunk to a cage of ribs on four scrawny legs; only her two flying ears had remained jaunty. On her last night, she had circled and bled, tottering against my waiting hands and willing her small body to keep fighting. At the vet's, I spoke softly to the small bundle in my arms but was shocked at how quickly her head flung back once the injection went in her vein. Taos had helped heal this loss. The womb of the Taos Mountains had been a fine remedy for my bruised spirit, and Little Bit had enjoyed the company of Angi's two feisty Chihuahuas.

It is good to return now and feel how the land receives me. At Angi's house, we sit outside throwing our wishes to the waiting stars and watching the moon climb over the mountain; when darkness extends her reach and nature takes over, my dear Idgie feels close in the warm winds and the howls of the lean coyote. I want to linger, want to delay my departure, want to push England into the furthest reaches of my life. But I know that my resistance is futile. I have always wanted my freedom from England, always wanted to be free of the past; going home now was the best and perhaps only way of achieving this.

Back in Colorado, Kim and I complete the slow business of sorting packs, washing clothes, and picking through our gritty food remnants. The hikes are already receding, the long journey on highways having replaced the steady rhythm of our feet. My thoughts are tending towards Madison, but there is one more person to see before I leave - a diminutive Iranian woman called Zari who is a friend and gifted psychic healer. It was Zari who had taught me the energy healing I used on my mother, and it was Zari who had once assured me that Madison could feel like home.

Her house looks ordinary enough, a suburban home tucked in

164

a housing complex on the south end of town, but it contains a great presence. When I arrive there in the heat of the day, the sun glints off her brick pathway and the whirly-gigs on the front lawn barely stir. I walk slowly down the stairs that lead to her office and push through the beaded curtains that tinkle like glass. Zari is there, an elfin figure seated behind a huge wooden desk.

"Julia," she cries. "I cannot believe you are leaving us."

She clasps me and then steps back, holding me lightly as if I were a jewel that she was turning towards the light.

"How are you, my dear?"

She rolls the last syllable, purring like a cat, and tears spring into my eyes. Behind her, bookshelves are lined with sacred texts and photographs of children with radiant eyes; to her left, framed diplomas tout her numerous skills. She leads me into the treatment room next door, a soothing place with a blue essence cast from hundreds of cobalt ornaments and wall hangings that are mostly gifts from clients. Her table, angled to a small window, puts me level with bottles of fragrant oil and beautiful stones. As she stands at my feet, lightly touching them to begin the session, she offers a simple prayer and a small tear of gratitude slides down my cheek.

As Zari begins her healing touch, ripples of energy move up and down my body. Places that were tight or emotionally strained begin to release. We speak a little about my return to England, and then, without knowing why, I tell her the story of the balcony and the scar across my right wrist; she touches it with feather hands. Suddenly, I am crying hard.

"I can't believe I still have emotion around this," I stammer. "I felt so scared and lonely that day when Michael shut me out on the balcony, but it was years ago. Why does it matter so much?"

"My dear," she answers softly, so softly that I begin to cry harder because of her compassion, "the scar touches all the way to the soul. We will take care of this," she says. "We will take care of this now."

She soothes on a level beneath her words; the place in me that grips that story lets go, talon-by-talon, and something close to compassion seeps in. When I open my eyes, I notice the stained glass plate that I gave Zari on a previous visit: it shows a fairy standing on

165

the tip of a dragonfly leaning out over water and almost losing her balance.

"You're just like her," Zari tells me. "I want to say to you look, look you are an angel, you have wings. You just need to use them."

When we hug goodbye, she touches her hand to her heart and sighs.

"I cannot believe you are really going," she says.

I take several chocolates from the small bowl on her desk. "For sustenance," I tell her, and she laughs. After one last look at everything in the room, I duck through the beaded curtain, climb the stairs and emerge into bright sunshine.

It is night when I reach Madison, Wisconsin and manoeuvre around the side of my former-girlfriend's house. In the back garden, I linger for a few minutes under the porch light. The rose bush transplanted from my first garden in Madison still blooms in one of the flowerbeds, and I can make out the edges of rhododendron and faded peony; a tree surrounded by hostas, where Little Bit likes to hide, has been blessed with some of Idgie's ashes.

Little Bit, of course, has heard the car wheels on the drive. When I open the back door quietly, using my own key, she barrels towards me across the wooden floor. I kneel and she flings herself, nose first, into the side of my neck and makes strange snuffling sounds. Patti appears, dressed in pyjamas, laughing and sleepy, her fair hair tousled; she offers me a warm hug.

"Welcome home," she says.

What really makes a home, I wonder? Is it the presence of those you love? Is it history? Is it small acts of caring like painting a wall or planting a garden? Sometimes it feels as if I have homes all over the place – as if a hologram of Julia peels off with each departure and remains in place. It is possible to meet myself over and over again.

Down in Patti's basement, the small meditation room still smells faintly of incense, and my red flannel sheets on the futon bed are comforting. Little Bit, momentarily confused about her sleeping loyalties, has finally left Patti's room on the first floor and followed me down here; it is good to have her warm body curled up next to mine.

Across the room, the large oak desk that now holds the television used to be the site of my dissertation struggles. Once, when the basement flooded, a wise friend suggested that the flood reflected my feelings of overwhelm at the sheer mass of academic knowledge. I had promptly returned more than ninety books to the library, and my relief had been palpable. I then refocused my project and began each chapter with an exploration of my own thoughts and feelings. The writing had flowed; after that, it was easier to ingest various books and theories and incorporate them without getting completely lost.

Still, it had been a constant struggle to integrate spiritual and emotional aspects of my life with academic work. Keeping them separate had felt artificial, and I admired people, such as my advisor, who managed to bring their deepest interests into their literary work. On the day of my dissertation defence, the final hurdle, I had cleaned the conference space, smudged it with sage, and placed sacred and familiar objects in all corners of the room. It had helped me feel grounded as I twirled and danced under the glare of the academic microscope.

But now, as I look back at the course of my life, Madison represents the maturing and eventual integration of my different aspects. I see a slow and steady process of building self. In the absence of a father's love, and in the cauldron of a mother's love coupled with anxiety, I had struggled to feel the substance of my being. It had been necessary to call back my imagination and encourage the subtle yet insistent shades of my emotions. From the time that I had left home, I had been discovering Julia from the ground up. There had been the shock and joy of first love, the awakening of my sexuality, the profound satisfaction of spiritual nourishment, the challenge of co-habitation, the lure of knowledge, the richness of soulful friendships, the wonders of the outdoors, and the pleasure of discovering my talents and natural inclinations.

Now, as I sink down into the flannel sheets and pull them up close under my chin, a sense of wellbeing rises in me. I nudge Little Bit further to one side, and she grunts and re-positions, temporarily willing to compromise. It will feel strange, emotional, to make my final goodbye with America; so much growth has happened here.

There are still things to release: old beliefs about England, patterns of control in family relationships, stray remnants of anger, and a habit of looking outside myself for approval. But in the depths of me, and now more frequently playing on the surfaces as well, there is an adamant vision of wholeness and a template of inner freedom that cannot be denied.

Slowly, reluctantly, I have peeled myself away from friends and from the land that has so patiently allowed me to grow at my own pace. As I bid goodbye to Patti, to the arboretum in full bloom, to the patch of woods grown familiar through dog walks, and to Idgie's ashes resting under the tree, the circle will gently close.

The work is done here; it is necessary to return to England and complete the story. I must integrate the past and the present; I am ready now. Although I have not admitted it to myself, I have been steadily pointing towards home.

PART THREE
RETURN

25

RETURN

I return home in style - passage for one human and one dog on the Queen Mary 2, a colossal yet elegant vessel that glides from New York to Southampton in just six days. It is Little Bit who has prompted this extravagance; she is far too precious to bundle into the hold of an airplane or expose to the careless whims of baggage handlers. And so it is that in late August 2008, we drive the nearly one thousand miles from Wisconsin to New York in three deliberate stages. Little Bit, perhaps not knowing the trip is in her honour, acts as if she would rather be anywhere than riding shotgun on the bags and trunks we have squeezed into my friend Marian's small blue Yarus. Each strange stop along the way, each noise from the busy highway, seems to imprint itself on Little Bit's resolute body.

On the final day of our journey, when we wind past desolate warehouses and trickle towards Brooklyn Harbour, Little Bit leans against the luggage, tongue extended, and peers out of the back window with the last vestiges of canine hope. We stop briefly to let her pee, but she rejects the inhospitable tarmac and dives into the shadows under the car. We coax her out, deposit her back in the red-checked dog bed, and drive the final few hundred feet. As we round the last corner, the Queen Mary 2 confronts us. Dubbed "the grandest most magnificent ocean liner ever built," her great black hulk looms out of the water and her elegant body, stacked with shining white cabins and red chimneys, preens into the sky.

We stop again to take a photograph and stand reverently in her shadow. She is, according to the ship's website, the length of forty-three double-decker London buses. Back in the car, Marion revs up to the terminal where a cluster of porters pluck bags, trunk, and bicycle from the car like a team of expert fruit pickers. I am left standing on the sidewalk, a forty-five-year-old woman clutching a dog bed, two backpacks, a laptop and Little Bit who is digging her claws into my arms. One minute Marion is hugging me goodbye, with Little Bit squeezed between us, and the next minute, I have shot through security and landed in the cavernous holding area. This is the no-man's land between places, the oddly exhilarating signifier for the end of one experience and the unknown possibilities of the next.

Ahead of me, check-in counters line up like a row of beach huts each staffed with smiling uniformed personnel. I aim in that direction, but before I can get there, an attendant intercepts and leads the way to a line of chairs over on one side. Dogs and their documents need to be processed before embarkation; we must wait.

"The purser will be along shortly," the woman tells me, bending down to pet Little Bit. "What's your dog's name? Little Bit? How cute."

I repeat this introduction at regular intervals as passengers and crew pass by. Some people stop to tell me about their dogs at home; a few people assume I am a fanatical pet owner unable to be apart from my dog, even on a cruise ship vacation that costs several thousand dollars. One man thrusts a video camera into our faces and asks if this is our first time on the Queen Mary. While I respond, Little Bit shrinks back and her tongue hangs further out of her mouth like the iconic Rolling Stones' album cover. Days later, the segment will appear looping endlessly in a video promotion on board the ship.

The wait drags on. Little Bit's breath is rank, and I have too many bags to go and find water. Someone waves an arm, dewlapped and laden with bracelets, and I recognize a German woman I had met quite recently in Madison. The Queen Mary 2 has a complicated dress code, and I had gone to Macey's department store with my friend, Deb, in search of the formal, semi-formal, formal-casual and casual dress mandated in the glossy brochure.

While I eased myself into a black-and-white dinner dress and

Deb planned my indoctrination into the world of patent leather shoes, we had chatted about the upcoming cruise. Our voices had carried. In a town that is miles from the coast, with a population topping two hundred thousand, we were sharing a changing area with a mother and daughter booked on the exact same cruise. The impossible odds had filled me with a sense of elation; it was a good omen, a sign that my return home after twenty-six years was indeed divinely guided.

The German woman exchanges a few friendly words, and then moves on, jewellery glinting like the plumage on an exotic bird. With my dog and my motley possessions, I am beginning to feel like a stowaway among this well-heeled crowd. It is a relief when the other dog people begin to arrive.

First comes a friendly young couple with a pacing German shepherd called Angus, and a black dog of mixed parentage known as Tilley who chases her tail and barks. Tilley is booked on the ship, but they are hoping Angus will be allowed to fill the empty slot caused by a last-minute cancellation. While they negotiate, a large bald man threads his way to our side of the room sweating profusely under the burden of two huge dog beds. I peer past him, expecting to see great Danes, but his wife appears carrying two self-assured longhaired miniature daschunds. These are definitely my kind of people; we are all in humble service to our dogs.

When the crisp white purser finally arrives, she scans the animals' microchips, checks records for correct vaccinations and blood work, and then hands us over to the kennel master. Darren, a slight Filipino man in grey uniform, gives us each a piece of paper, like a secret mantra, with typed instructions for kennel visiting hours. Then, he holds out his arms and offers to take Little Bit on board.

"Can't I carry her on?" I ask, dismayed at the thought of handing her off like a piece of luggage.

"Of course," he answers with a slight bow. "Please follow me."

Those of us with small dogs follow Darren, a ragged bunch offering up a comical contrast to the phalanx of eight uniformed staff members lined up on either side of the ship's entrance. Behind their bobbing heads and smiles, rich red carpet leads to sweeping stairways, a circle of expensive shops, and a lower lobby with highly polished elevator doors. We walk through, dogs held high, and ride one of these elevators up to the twelfth floor. There, we pile out on to a small landing and exit through a heavy metal door onto the upper deck.

Fresh air greets us, a relief after the thick atmosphere of perfumes and lotions that swirls around the bevy of female passengers on board. Our dogs may have simple housing, but they are on the most desired level of the ship. Their concrete home sits at the rear of the vessel and over to one side. It will be a distinct pleasure to visit Little Bit and gaze out across the water once we have launched; the dog area will be as much our home on the ship as it is theirs. As we enter the enclosed deck area, where they will exercise and relieve themselves, we laugh at a large red sign that reads: "Danger: These Animals May Bite."

Inside the small building that will house seven dogs on this transatlantic trip, a double row of cages provides accommodation for small dogs on top and big dogs below. Little Bit will spend her nights suspended above two elderly boxers and cheek by jowl with the daschunds, Mia and Gromit. She is not excited by this prospect. While I unpack her tins of prescription dog food, she glances around uneasily. I warn Darren that Little Bit is wary of being lifted and then demonstrate the best way to get her into the cage. She cowers at the clang of the metal door and stares at me through the mesh.

"Good girl," I tell her. "I'll be back really soon. It's okay."

Little Bit looks scared but trusting. I stay just long enough to hear David, the bald man, negotiate extra visiting hours for Mia and Gromit, who need regular medication, and then I leave her; I go back through the metal door and descend, this time, via the red-carpeted stairs.

My room, six floors below Little Bit, is cave-like and snug with twin beds; shower and vanity; writing desk; small circular dining table and chair; tiny refrigerator and more closet space than I will get at my mother's cottage. Unlike the State Rooms on the upper decks, regular cabins are windowless and lined up like monk's cells to provide a significant portion of the ship's accommodation. At capacity, the Queen Mary 2 can house more than three thousand guests. Replete with swimming pools, hot tubs, exercise rooms, restaurants, bars, theatres and casino she is a grand hotel on the water.

Now that the complicated part of my journey is over, I stretch out on my narrow bed and close my eyes. Luggage, identified by a graded system of coloured tags, arrives in fits and starts and is delivered to our doors by an army of porters who swarm the corridors like ants. Mercifully, one of these porters suggests taking my bike to the hold, since the spare bed is already piled with luggage and my room is beginning to feel like a storage closet. There was no limit to the number of bags I could bring, and I have interpreted this quite liberally. With my belongings stowed, the sounds of the scurrying porters and the voices of guests passing back and forth lull me into a light and restless sleep.

When I wake, the ship is still not moving, although the engines throb like a colony of bees. It is time to feed Little Bit, and when I return to the top deck and release her from captivity, she is thrilled. She clings, back legs trembling, breathing in hot gasps on my neck.

All the owners are there in the cordoned off enclosure watching their animals and comparing notes. While the dogs get acquainted through various sensory organs, we monitor intake and output like a brood of anxious hens. Has Little Bit peed yet? What happens if she needs to go once she is back in her cage? If she doesn't poop could it be dangerous? Darren reassures us; most dogs take a day or two to adjust, and it takes that long for them to get used to peeing and pooping on wooden slats. Still, we perform a charade of verbal and physical encouragement, dragging our dogs up and down the deck hoping that one of them will lift a leg or squat. When the dam finally breaks, we celebrate.

It is early evening when the Queen Mary finally eases out of Brooklyn Harbour, but the launch is so smooth, or my focus on getting into evening dress so acute, that it happens without my knowledge. My main concern is navigating from my cabin to dinner at a dignified pace. Hampered by high-heeled shoes, I mince down to the formal dining area allocated to my particular class of travel; I am grateful for the cushion of thick carpet and the presence of tables and chairs. As I weave towards my assigned table, two elderly gentlemen stand politely and bid me welcome. We introduce ourselves, and Stephen bustles off to fetch a bottle of wine from his cabin with an eagerness that belies his years. A quick glance around the room assures me that choosing the early dining hour has put me in the class of families and octogenarians.

The evening proceeds with friendly formality; we eat our food with delicate precision and drink our wine in measured sips. The men are neighbours in Toronto, well used to each other's company, and grateful for fresh ears. Stephen, the more vocal of the two, has recently lost his wife, and the trip is coloured by her absence, revealed in his fond stories and conveyed by his wistful face. As I listen, gazing surreptitiously over their heads at the elegant diners and the timed flourishes of crisp middle-aged waiters, the Queen Mary moves steadily away from port.

By the time I leave the dining area and return to my cabin for more comfortable clothes, we are well out to sea. Out on deck, the air is bracing. As the ship forges on, lighting a path along the water, the distant clink of glasses and muffled voices tune to the background hum of the engines and the slapping of water against the ship's sides.

At the dog run, most people are dressed for the late dinner sitting. David, alone, wears shorts. He has come without formal wear and tells me that not one of the ship's rental jackets will fit his power lifter's physique. I envy his freedom; the jackets would only pinch his shoulders and pinion his wings. For while I had sat decorously dining, the corks on the champagne bottles had popped on deck, the guests had cheered, and glasses has been lifted to the last glimpse of Liberty, torch upraised, disappearing on the New York skyline.

26

I sleep soundly in my windowless cabin, barely feeling the swell and pitch of the ship because of its size and the clement weather. When I visit Little Bit, she too has survived her first night well. On my arrival, she yawns, stretches and does her business out on deck, dodging the upset stomachs of two of her canine companions. While Darren swabs the deck, sending the waste into a holding area below, she trots around, sniffs the sea air, and then sits contentedly on my lap looking out at the expanse of water beyond the wooden railing.

My days take shape around these visiting hours and the pleasures of being on deck. Guests of various nationalities ignore the warning sign and lean over the gate to the dog enclosure; they stroke the dogs and speak longingly of animals left behind. Even the Captain's wife makes a daily visit, and our corner of the ship becomes an alternate social scene. Little Bit treats all this attention with nonchalance. She is also unmoved by photo sessions in her complementary Cunard jacket or the bright orange life vest monogrammed with "Outward Hound." She is focused mainly on my presence or absence and on her regular daily feeds.

Although we have formed a tight-knit group, diminished slightly when Angus nips one of the elderly Boxers, my status as solitary traveller sets me apart. Most of the ship's guests and all of the dog owners are couples. When we share stories, they speak confidently of their concrete plans or their waiting jobs. It is harder to describe my return - my need to map my father's absence or the urge to see England in a new light. I am returning to the place of constraint in order to find freedom, and that is hardly a template for cruise ship conversation.

But one morning, as I am reflecting on my solitude, two women approach the dog area. The taller one, fair and slightly patrician, has a white denim jacket over her cotton trousers. The other, dark-haired and scrappy like an eager terrier, has a loose yellow t-shirt hanging over calf-length blue-and-white striped trousers. They are not typical of this cruise ship's guests.

"Hi!" the dark-haired one says. "Can we see your dog?"

They are right at the edge of the barrier, so I lift Little Bit and we talk across her eleven-inch body.

"How is your cruise going so far?" asks Shari, the dark-haired one.

"It's not really my scene," I tell her. "I am just here because of Little Bit."

Shari frowns, and her voice takes on the tone of an older friend or a sister who won't take any nonsense from you.

"It's not our 'scene' either," she challenges me, "but that doesn't mean you can't enjoy it. This is a transatlantic crossing; this is how people used to travel. It is amazing."

As she speaks of earlier crossings, and the way a ship's slow passage makes you aware of the vast distances between peoples, her animated face matches her eloquence. She paints scenes with a characteristic American enthusiasm, and I secretly admire the way she has put me in my place. Her partner, Celia, is more reserved. She seems used to Shari's blunt speech and hangs back, observing. They move on, leaning into each other and laughing, and my solitary status seem even more acute. I resolve to follow Shari's advice and take advantage of the things on offer; with a rather grim determination, English style, I resolve to enjoy myself.

My first stop is the gym, located through the elegant spa, where I spend thirty minutes pounding on a treadmill in a row of earnest women. This is followed by yoga on the mats. By the time I have showered and changed, the acting class taught by fresh-faced students from the Royal Academy of Dramatic Arts is just beginning. They lead us in warm-ups, mime, and improvisation on the polished floor of the Grand Ballroom, while the ship's video team solemnly records the event.

The day wears on, and when evening falls, buoyed by the complementary sparkling wine, I peruse the glossy supplement left on my pillow each night by the Filipino maid. Maribel, who performs this service, as well as turning down the covers and keeping the cabins clean, has told me about her daughter back in the Philippines whom she sends money to but barely sees. Darren has a similar story, although his first child has not yet been born. He will probably miss the birth, because he will most likely be somewhere at sea catering to the whims of travellers who must transport their dogs.

The contrast between these lives and the opulence on board ship creates an uneasy feeling that stays with me while I change into the requisite formal-casual clothes and go to the auditorium for the after-dinner show. For my last act, I sink into one of the plush red seats and listen to the off-Broadway star belt out show tunes in her long glittering dress.

Shari and Celia rescue me from these forced activities. We bump into each other at breakfast the next morning, where they are taking photographs of their laden plates and the decoratively carved watermelons placed strategically around the buffet. They are New Yorkers, as much at home with farce as with intellectual banter, and we ease into conversation and familiarity as if we have known each other a long time.

As the days unfold, we will enjoy hot tubs, long conversations in their balcony suite with room service, and intense games of paddle tennis. They are interested in history, and we visit the wood-panelled library where they ferret out information on the ship and take pictures of the poster that shows an up-ended Queen Mary stretching higher than the Eiffel Tower. Maps also fascinate them, and we study the ones framed on the walls, especially the one showing the route of the Titanic and its precise sinking point. They drag me to the bridge, and we peer through the glass, laughing about the tiny wheel used for steering when the ship comes off autopilot.

In the evenings, we take pictures of each other in our evening dresses; Celia's elegant gown has been borrowed from a friend, but the velvet robe that Shari wears doubles as her Halloween costume. They join me for two formal dinners and entertain the elderly gentlemen at my table with talk of opera, art and World War II.

Although I taste the distinct pleasures of this light-hearted company and long for it to continue, my journey home remains a solitary one. At the heart of this return, my mother waits patiently in her Sussex cottage. We are linked, despite our geographical distance, by the invisible threads that make mother and daughter feel each other's emotions and forget they are not responsible for each other's happiness or despair. She is part of what made me leave, and she is part of what makes me return. Coming home now is a small deposit set against my long absence, inevitable somehow, as if the energy I had spent repudiating England had simply amassed somewhere; the force that catapulted me out at eighteen was now drawing me home, as if I was always only on the end of a piece of elastic stretching, stretching to its tense, quivering end point until it snapped back.

Alone on deck, looking out across the vast body of undefined water that mirrors the vacancy and possibility of my return, the smooth, leaping backs of porpoise or dolphin taunt me with their freedom. If I could just change old habits, unwind myself from stories that cling, then this smooth leaping passage through the water could be mine.

But leaving is easier than the return. My maternal grandmother, for instance, left her native Australia at twenty-one and sailed to England. She trusted that her life with a benevolent aunt in Wales would be better than her existing one. Perhaps she had become bored of the wide-open spaces, the shimmering heat, the long droughts, and the rough company of ranchers on the sheep farm where she grew up. Or maybe she longed for the kind of attention that being one of six children with a new stepmother could not provide.

Whatever the mix of reasons, my grandmother hatched a plan, wrote to the childless aunt in Wales, and secured passage on a boat. Whether she left with her father's blessing or in secret, she boarded the ship alone and turned her face away from the vast dryness of Australia towards the rainy sliver of land that would be her new home. In the same year that Australia officially became a Commonwealth country, Harriet Mary Kelly began a whole new life.

I can imagine her sense of freedom as she ended her life in

182

Australia with forty-plus days and nights steaming across the Indian Ocean and up into the chillier Atlantic stream. I can resonate with her passion for a new life. Sailing to a new home takes raw courage, and at eighteen or twenty-one there is plenty to spare. But sailing back to the familiar requires something different: a true knowledge of who you were and who you have become.

The last night on board the Queen Mary passes swiftly. My new friends order room service in their balcony suite. We linger over dinner and, once Little Bit is tucked up for the night, meet up for an outdoor hot tub. As we sit in the steamy water and watch the churning of the ship's wake, we talk lightly about the past week and their onward journey to the final stop at Hamburg. But I am light-headed from wine and the anticipation of landing, and the hot water makes me feel faint. We call it a night quite early and shuffle back to our respective cabins in white towelling robes and Cunard slippers. As we pass along the corridors, several women in full evening gowns shrink back as if our informality might be catching. Safe in my cabin, hollowed out and dry like a walnut shell, I finish my packing and go to bed alone.

My alarm goes off before daylight. On deck, a slight drizzle announces the English morning. Seagulls wheel and turn overhead and tiny boats bob on the horizon. The ship feels smaller and my stomach tighter, as if the insides are pulling away from the outer skin. The boat shudders, and in the eerie first light we slide into Southampton among the mud flats. There is no elegant skyline here, and no statue of hope and freedom. Under the chill stare of warehouses, the cottages on the far shore huddle together for warmth and giant cranes lift steel heads into a cold sky.

Shari and Celia say goodbye under the lifeboats on the seventh floor deck. The rain patters lightly and the ominous sky casts shadow. We make grim jokes about the weather and then embrace. As Shari hugs me, she speaks low into my ear, and her words reverberate.

"All decisions are reversible, you know."

27

PAST, PRESENT AND FUTURE

Some decisions are not reversible. Some you learn to live with like a memory that won't go away or a scar on the back of your hand that persists in a slightly raised yet faded line.

On the deck of the Queen Mary on this overcast day, Little Bit's papers are checked and approved, remaining dollars handed over to Darren, and then the slow orderly process of disembarkation begins. Little Bit seems reluctant to leave her temporary home, and she resists joining the line of people filing out of the doors. She must be coaxed and then carried as we exit the ship across a gangplank, walk down covered corridors, and emerge into a vast echoing warehouse filled with people and luggage. Every cry and shout echoes off the corrugated walls, and Little Bit scrabbles against my body like a fox going to ground. I move forward slowly, backpacks and dog covering me like a straightjacket.

At the far end of the warehouse, a row of signs indicates each cabin class and offers a clue to the whereabouts of one's particular luggage. In contrast to the careful delivery system at embarkation, it looks as if the great ship has belched out bags with a satisfied sigh at reaching her destination. I hail the youngest looking porter who stands patiently while I ferret out my possessions. He loads them, trunk at the bottom, in an ungainly pile on his dolly; they totter dangerously, until he tips the dolly at a forty-five degree angle and waits while a burly ship's officer goes in search of my bike. When we finally wheel towards the exit, with me pushing my bike and carrying Little Bit under one arm, it is Michael, once again, who stands waiting at the barrier.

He is the one who has never left, the contained yet steady presence in my mother's life, as if our father had entrusted her to their first-born. He is here for me too; I feel that now, even though our ways of seeing the world can be quite different, and the past sometimes flares up like a bushfire. If anyone, besides my mother, is to feel the effects of my return it will be him; the balance and spread of filial duty will be radically altered. It feels right; he has shouldered the responsibility that physical proximity demands for quite some time.

"Please could you give the porter a generous tip? I don't have any English money with me, and he was really patient. I had way more luggage than anyone else."

"You're telling me," Michael replies. "At the barrier, some bloke made fun of all the luggage Americans bring on holiday. I had to confess that my sister had all that *and* a bike and a dog. It's a good thing I came alone; it will only just fit in the car."

I think longingly of fourteen boxes of books, kitchen implements and framed pictures that are stored with friends. The furniture went in yard sales months before, and the final act had been selling my car. Possessions cannot define you, but they do offer comfort. Contrary to my brother's impression, I have come home with relatively little, but my life outside England does not register here.

Our drive east from Southampton and then slightly north to Lurgashall in West Sussex takes under two hours. Even though the time change has been gradual, we had moved clocks forward one hour for each day of our passage, my body feels languid, as if I am jet lagged or recovering from flu. Perhaps it is the swell of the ocean still present in my system or the physical recognition that my move has really taken place.

Yet as we enter the Sussex countryside, dislocation shifts into a quiet appreciation for the country lanes, the luminescent arch of beech trees, and the verdant greens of growing crops interspersed with splashes of rapeseed yellow. There is a simple tranquillity here and my body registers this.

I am entering my mother's territory, but it feels familiar as if her work of connection has also created a link for me. In the sixteen years that my mother has been in Lurgashall, she has made a home among the people and surrounding nature. She lives on a quiet road a stone's throw from the shop, church and pub that offer focal points for her small community. She is halfway between the village green and the council estate, a position that perfectly reflects her ability to reach across class divides in small yet meaningful ways. She is a fixture at village lunches, makes up fifty percent of the church choir on sparse Sundays, and is forever baking cakes for this tea or that fête.

She is also in constant dialogue with her garden. Wearing her green Wellington boots, and with foam kneelers attached to the outside of her trousers, she is often ensconced in some corner where she weeds, edges, turns earth, moves plants, and thins out dense areas in her carefully arranged beds. Hers is a well-tended garden, although the battle with weeds is ongoing and the daisies seem to spring back as if they had simply moved aside for the electric mower.

Some days, my mother trundles her wheelbarrow and tools down the road to an allotment behind the village shop. There, she prepares the earth and sows lines of seed marked with tiny plastic strips that sometimes get muddled, so that lettuce becomes parsley or spinach turns into kale. But despite this, her small patch at the scruffier end holds its own among the immaculately tended, wooden-edged plots of the more fanatical gardeners. It is these simple pleasures that I enjoy.

As the car makes the last turn into her drive, all seems in its usual place. As if she has sensed my imminent arrival, my mother is standing outside her front door. Her hair is completely white but her face relatively unlined. She is wearing loose linen trousers, and one hip rises higher than the other, as if she has become accustomed to uneven ground. Little Bit, relieved perhaps to feel grass under her paws instead of wooden slats, trots off to explore.

As I walk towards my mother, she simply raises her arms and enfolds me, crying softly and clutching me to her as if I am something precious that had been lost and is now returned. It does not matter that I was here earlier in the year. For both of us, this is my real return; the boat-ride was a one-way passage home.

Once we disentangle, I drag my bulky suitcases up the narrow stairs of my mother's cottage towards the spare bedroom where she has placed a small bouquet of garden flowers. A memory hits me: I was home from boarding school, and she put flowers in my room. Cruelly, I made her take them away; I did not want to receive anything from her that would require an open heart.

Through the window, the apple tree hangs heavy with fruit, and a birds' nest, balanced in its branches, has layer upon layer of intricate sticks. Little Bit appears and disappears below; she is inspecting her new territory, sniffing out evidence of cats like a marshal and using her nose to overturn dry leaves.

Far away, the lunch preparations are going on without me, and Michael has resumed organizing the garden shed. He does this each time he visits, restless until he has lined up the jumble of watering cans, spray bottles, empty pots, and tools. He does not always consult my mother, however, and occasionally piles things in front of shelves, causing her to lean and grope when reaching for the slug bait or the fertilizer. Still, he is a master at making things appear neat and orderly.

Restoring order is a trait several of us in the family share. Back in May, before I knew about the shed's continually fluctuating state, I tidied as if I imagined it would stay that way. While Mum mowed the lawn one afternoon, whipping the cord of her electric mower out of harm's way with each stripe of the lawn, I emptied the shed, swept the old floorboards, and wiped away some of the cobwebs from the walls. Together, we sorted the piles on the lawn and jettisoned items that she had not used for decades.

We made a good job of it, removing piles of mouse-eaten gloves, recycling an old grass container on wheels and relocating scores of empty lawn and fertilizer bags. Re-filling the shed had been easy, and I took great pains to leave a clear path to the shelves and created a protected space in anticipation of my bike's arrival later that summer. It had been premature. Long before I returned, the shed had been rendered chaotic and cleaned numerous times.

A light rain begins to fall, making its "tap-tap" on the conservatory roof and mocking the parched geraniums. I will sleep in this room tonight, but tomorrow I will move to the empty bedroom on the other side of the cottage. This will be my fresh start. It is a smaller room, but the window looks out over the bird feeder, and there is a particular pineapple broom tree that the birds love. I will place my desk under that window, and watching the birds hop and preen each morning will be my particular delight.

Just now, the wood pigeons are calling loudly. They are lined up along the telephone cable that stretches across the garden, and their cooing reminds me of summers at Brown House where the pigeons kept up a constant commentary. It is strange to think of it being torn down, eviscerated from living memory except for the name that still survives in rusty lettering at the top of a five-bar gate.

I was eleven when he made our final visit to Brown House in September 1974. In my last entry in the Visitors' Book, after the usual report on how I had spent my time, I made several suggestions about preparing the house for its new owners: prise up splinters on the slide, put spiders in the sheets, add lipstick on brushes, create water spurting flowers, and dot the mirrors with red spots to make people look as if they are ill. "Now you know what to do if *your* house is being sold," I had declared, to no one in particular. Apparently, I had been unaware that the house would be knocked down; there would be no one to play on the slide, no one to look in mirrors, and no one to smell the flowers or sleep in the beds.

28

"We'll never find a parking space. The theatre begins in twenty minutes."

"Visualize one," I tell my mother.

We are in the market town of Guildford, Surrey one week into my return and cruising the tightly packed rows of a slim-line car park tucked between the river and the road. We are going to the Yvonne Arnaud Theatre for a matinee presentation. At the perfect moment, a car backs out of a space and my mother's Renault slips easily into the small vacant berth. We walk the short distance to the theatre and join the crowd of pensioners sipping cups of coffee and tea.

At the five-minute warning bell, my mother confesses she needs one of the theatre's hearing aids and walks diffidently over to the counter.

"Which one do you need?" a young man asks cheerily. "The loop or the standard?"

"Oh, I don't know. This one will do."

Inside the auditorium, the lights dim and the expectant hush of any theatre dissipates in the rustles and whispers of this older crowd. The play commences. Billed as a light and quintessential British comedy, to my half-American ears it is surprisingly dark. Incest lines get laughs and the crowd warms to a caricature of self-deprecating Englishness, as if this trait were indeed a national treasure. It all feels too close to the bone. The protagonist is a son who lives with his ageing mother in a tumbledown home. She speaks to her television and refuses any technological updates, while he lives in his own world and talks to his cats. There are lines in the play that sound uncannily like things my mother and I would say.

It is clear from her delayed reactions and puzzled looks that my mother is not getting any of this. At the interval, she admits that she is hearing very little but refuses to get the other kind of hearing aid.

"You just have to expect this kind of thing when you get old," she says.

When we leave the theatre, sidestepping shuffling bodies, we take the steep cobbled road to the centre of town. In a newsagent's, my mother hovers and makes it difficult for me to choose my brother's birthday card; I am relieved when she goes across the street in search of shoes.

When our shopping is finished, we start walking towards the car park, cutting through a side street that leads to a flight of steep stairs and then a narrow passage. A woman appears at the far end. There is room for two abreast, but she waits for us to come through. The same impulse stirs in my mother, and she hurries because she does not want to make the woman wait. In this flurry of politeness, she almost tumbles headfirst down the stairs.

Such signs of Englishness feel distant and strange, more so now that I am living here. Although the behaviour seems merely considerate, there is an anxiety attached to it that stirs my impatience. When you shift geography, you shift your habits, your inclinations, your temperament; you take on the shape and flavour of what is around you. How will I translate myself, and what new language will I learn in order to be understood? Everywhere I go in England, people think I am American. I have absorbed an accent and a way of speaking that will not leave despite the smiles, comments and corrections.

At a book signing, weeks from now, a brilliant Scottish writer will compliment me on my woollen hat and inquire where I am from.

"I'm English," I will tell her; she will laugh.

"Well, where did you get that accent from then? You have dual nationality; that is a gift."

A dual identity is the writer's position as well, simultaneously living and observing, as if splitting oneself into two. It is also what makes it possible to tell my mother I am "just passing through," and so preserve the feeling of my choice and freedom. In my diary, I record shifting emotions, illusionary fears of being trapped, and the resistances that have made me push against England in the past like an angry child.

"Stop blaming England," a friend admonishes. But why does being happy here feel like such a concentrated task?

Writing, as always, offers a way of soothing by putting it all outside me as text. A writer flirts with experience and caresses words until observation becomes a fierce and tender intimacy with life.

When my mother was eighty, she walked ten miles on her daughter-in-law's fiftieth birthday, because a group was going to a particular pub in the New Forest where they were staying. She kept up a good pace, using a walking stick for purchase on the soft, springy ground. But the next day, she moved around at a hobble; her knees ached and the soles of her feet were bone. I wrote a poem – a distillation of love that poured back to me through the images and the memory of her tired legs and feet.

But there is a danger. It is possible to observe too much and experience too little. I do not want to miss the sweetness of my mother's company or the spurt of laughter that hits my chest at the feeling of being known and loved. We make bread together. She stands on one side of the kitchen table with an apron on measuring flour, butter, yeast and salt into the mixing bowl; I write the recipe down. She gives tips on the proportion of brown flour to white and then shows me how to mix the butter in with my fingers. She confesses that she really prefers lard, in fact has used lard most of her life, but she knows that I prefer butter.

As I write down the precise measurement of warm water, Mum fills a jug with a random amount and adds it according to intuition.

"How would you describe this consistency?" I ask.

"You just have to feel it really," she replies.

I wash my hands, put on an apron and assume Mum's position in front of the mixing bowl. The dough feels warm and springy.

"I usually mix for five minutes by hand, and then a further five by electric mixture," she tells me.

"I am going to do the whole ten minutes by hand."

I plunge down and bring up sticky handfuls that I fold back

into the remaining mixture, repeating the action over and over in a pleasing, steady rhythm.

"You look good making bread," my mother remarks.

When the dough is ready, she shows me how to oil a bag and cover the bowl so the uncooked bread can rise. We leave it, quietly ascending on top of the stove where it is warm and draft-free. Within thirty minutes, the mixture has come all the way to the top of the bowl and threatens to spill over. We peel off the bag, beat the dough back down, and knead until it is ready to go into the tins. As we fill them evenly and put them into the hot oven, my mother tells me that my father used to enjoy baking bread rolls.

"Really?" I say. "I had never imagined him cooking."

"He used to make special shapes for Michael and call up the stairs to announce the arrival of, or receive orders for, a fresh batch of what he called Tolls or Ptolemy Newts."

I picture this intimate scene, quite outside my own experience of a father.

"The kitchen would be in such a mess when he had finished – flour everywhere," my mother adds.

We smile, both remembering how I used to cook as a little girl when I would "treat" my mother to surprise breakfasts; afterwards, the kitchen would look as if a tornado had hit. Perhaps I had inherited this trait.

When Michael reads this part of the manuscript, he remembers making the rolls and urges me to make more of the fact that they were named after philosophers. What do I make of this? Was my father interested in astronomy? Did he place his faith in the movement of stars and the natural laws governing the earth and the celestial bodies? Or, like Ptolemy, was he fated to map his world using fallible co-ordinates?

We need guides, familiars, signs and places in the landscape that connect us to a larger story. Perhaps my father had none of these. When I walk the moonscapes of moles and rabbits, the paths that my mother has trod for sixteen years, I am literally walking in her footsteps. And there is a tree down a shady lane that for years she would visit whenever she thought of her children. If she was worried about one of us and wanted to feel reassured, she would put her hands on the sturdy trunk of this tree and pray. If I were to place my hands there now, surely I would feel her.

And in the same way that I long for and love the taste of my mother's brown bread, Michael lusts after her marmalade. He looks forwards to late January or February, when Seville oranges appear in the stores, knowing that my mother will pull out her large steel pot and boil up a tangy mixture of fruits and peels. She calls him when the first batch of marmalade is lined up on the top of her kitchen cupboard, sure that he will visit her and take several precious jars. Then he will call in a day or two, reporting back about taste and texture - this batch is good, that batch a little runny or too coarsely cut.

These are the comforting aspects of home - the safe things like endless games of cards or scrabble. My mother and I take refuge here when we are tired or when tempers fray. A quick card game can sometimes bring balance more effectively than words, and a contest of scrabble is tantamount to saying sorry or enacting a truce. There is comfort in the ritual of sliding letters into the bag at the end of the game, tucking away the wooden letter pews with the board, and closing the tattered cardboard box for another day.

Jigsaws puzzles meet a different need; they offer a more prolonged distraction. When my mother hunches her body over the green baize table that holds pieces of a jigsaw, she becomes obsessed and fascinated enough to neglect dusting, vacuuming, exercise or anything else that gets in the way of completing the picture that forms under her fingers. There is a certain relaxation associated with this; it is a complete break from routine that has the ultimate effect of re-focusing my mother's mind.

I have learned to dip in and out of this particular pursuit, particularly since we have such different styles and approaches to puzzle making. My mother works from the colour and pattern, with only occasional reference to the picture on the box. She has so many pieces out it is hard to see the emerging shapes, and as she leans over the board, moving from one quadrant to another at random, her sleeve often catches on stray bits of the puzzle. I am forever diving under the table or pointing out pieces that have clung to her sweater or been tracked into another corner of the room.

My approach to puzzles is more focused, deliberate, and unrelenting. I find the unusual pieces and work exclusively on one corner, referring to the larger picture until it is clear where the pieces belong. Our different styles mean that we work best in shifts; we engage and then withdraw, settling ourselves behind a book, a project or a closed door. The space is necessary, yet the subtle consciousness of each other's presence beats steadily and will outlive the grave.

When the rich smell of baking fills the cottage and the timer goes off, we empty the tins, return the bread to the oven to bake off the base, and then line them up on a wire tray. The first taste with butter is divine; my mother declares it an excellent batch.

Will it be these memories that linger? Will I stand in a kitchen years from now and repeat these steps, the physical act of bread-making collapsing time and distance so that my mother feels alive long after she is dead?

29

LOVE

Wherever we love there is comfort. These skies, trees and hedgerows are now my daily companions and water speaks eloquently through narrow streams and rain-filled clouds.

If you turn left out of my mother's cottage and follow the road down past the millpond, there is a shady lane that runs next to a field. Across the field, you will find a small patch of woodland that becomes a sea of bluebells each spring; now, in late summer, it is the rich emerald of beech one notices and the patterns of sunlight filtering through the leaves.

One evening at dusk, when I am walking through the field towards the woodland, a young deer lifts her startled head; we seem to lock eyes. When she leaps and bounds away, her tense, trembling acuity stays with me. Closer to the woods, where the older trees creak and the slender trunks moan and sway, a young badger startles me in the long grass. In the woodland, a sett hides in the turning bracken - a city of shy animals detectable only through footprints and a faint musky smell. The badger must be coming to or from his home. He bristles his bold white stripe then takes a detour and ducks through a hole in the hedge, hastening away in his odd shambling gait. Deer and badger: they are both healers, each of a different kind. One is gentle, one aggressively determined; both are necessary in this excavation of mine.

The past moves in my body. Sometimes, I dream about our old house, and fragments of memory rise to the surface like hollow bone. Daydreaming is something different; I can walk through the rooms of the old house and choose my experiences. Here is where I accidentally kicked my foot through the glass bedroom door in a rage. There is the balcony where Michael locked me out. In the bathroom, a plaque contains a rhyme about proper etiquette for bathing and water use, a rhyme I still remember, and in my mother's bedroom closet, I see the set of wooden shelf dividers where she kept her socks and stockings. Downstairs in the kitchen, Susie, our Labrador, has a big wooden bed on legs.

Once, when my mother went down the road to visit her friend, Rosemary, I got scared in the night and curled up on a thin mattress next to that big wooden bed. A dog gives comfort just by being. When Idgie lay dead in my arms, after the vet had administered the injection, there was such gratitude mixed with the sorrow; how could this small body house such love? In Arizona, the ground is too hard for burial, and if the grave is shallow, the coyotes come; Idgie stayed with me for several days, kept in a small box in the freezer. By the time I drove her over a hundred miles to the crematorium in Tempe, we had said our goodbyes. It was a complete acceptance of love and loss.

My mother said goodbye to her friend Rosemary in the same graceful way. For forty years they had given each other love and counsel despite their different parenting styles. When Rosemary was dying of cancer, I drove my mother to Herefordshire, and we visited the hospital. It was a surprise visit. I went in first, ready with stories of recent hikes in the Brecon Becons, but the sight of Rosemary stemmed my tongue. This woman who had always been engaged in worthy work was now inactive, her skin tinged yellow and her face painfully pinched. Gratitude welled up close to the sorrow, for she had loved me as a second mother would.

When I left the room and made way for my mother to enter, the two of them let out a simultaneous primal cry. Rosemary had not expected her, might even have discouraged her visit, but was so palpably pleased that she had come. My mother cried. As I closed the door behind me, she laid her grieving head on Rosemary's swollen feet.

These are the easier deaths – the ones that come at the right time. My father's death demands something more: my father's choice to kill himself requires that we accept his human sovereignty even in the face of our devastating loss.

When I studied Journalism as an undergraduate in Colorado, I used some of my assignments to research and understand depression. One of the men I interviewed, on hearing my personal connection to the subject, volunteered to answer any of my questions; he had struggled with depression most of his life. As we talked, he conveyed how deadening depression is, how it can steal your will to live, and how recent advances in medicine had literally saved his life. He did his best to convey the utter blackness that my father might have felt. Years later, I would gain more insight into the horror and loneliness of depression when I read Kay Redfield Jamison's vulnerable account in *The Unquiet Mind*.

It is this combination of intellectual and emotional exploration that satisfies my need; knowledge gives structure for feeling, but facts are not enough if there is a small child lodged inside who is furious, sad, or abandoned. You have to reach in and offer comfort to all those different aspects of yourself; the years in Madison had been good for that.

Now, by coming home, I had brought with me all the experiences, insights and attitudes from the kibbutz, the ashram, and the years spent in America; I had laid these down as stories set on top of old ones like geological strata. In the points that touch and in the writing, new stories seem possible; they step forth from the inner and outer landscape bearing the lines and marks of all those layers.

On a sunny Saturday in mid-September, I cross the Hog's Back and drive into Hampshire, wending my way through Winchester's one-way system and slowing down by the statue of Alfred the Great - the same statue pictured on my father's schoolboy diary. Such was the silence surrounding him, that during four years of boarding school, I never once made the explicit connection that my father had lived and studied in the same town as me more than thirty years before.

When I reach the all-girls' boarding school, perched above Winchester like a decorative button, the afternoon lacrosse matches announced on the slick new website have long been over. Instead of a bustle of parents and players, I am faced with a ghost town. It is deathly quiet and feels uncannily like a stage set where the actors and directors are on break. Weekends were always like this; daygirls and weekly boarders fled, leaving the school an empty husk with only the housemistresses and the full-time boarders clinging to its sides.

At the threshold, I slow down and breathe. It all looks the same: the driveway with its aisle of trees, the rectangular brick buildings, the arched windows, and the clock hovering above the unknown Latin school motto.

I drive slowly over the speed bumps, and then a one-way system forces me past the long brick building that was my boarding house and back up the next driveway to a car park near the tennis courts. These have been re-surfaced since my day, and the area next to them, where we used to play house lacrosse matches, has now become a forecourt for a whole new set of buildings. Next to the car park, an indoor swimming pool has apparently replaced the old one that lay exposed on the high Hampshire hill.

At the back of the school, the main assembly room is concealed behind thick curtains, and the bike shed has gone. I had liked the bike shed; it had seemed out of place, ramshackle, and a soft contrast to the flat red brick. A woman waves uncertainly from the new dining room; I wave back. It is important to look confident for the new CTV cameras aimed from every building onto the empty paths.

To my right, the back door of my old boarding house is still a faded blue and the paint is peeling. No one has bothered to give it a fresh look. Behind it, there is probably the same small changing-room and the same row of hard enamel basins. I pause to feel, but the memory has little impact. I had anticipated a reaction – a need for release or the consecration of unhallowed ground. But all I feel is a calm indifference; the past has already been healed.

At the front of the school, a teenage girl sits on the grass waiting. She is not in uniform, so perhaps she is a weekly border about to return home. In the old days, trips off school grounds were rare and rendered uncomfortable by our brown tweed uniform. Mandatory church and occasional shopping were allowed, but wandering was discouraged; a walk to the local sweet shop required verbal permission, one's signature in a book, and adherence to various rules.

"Hello. I used to go to this school."

She smiles politely.

"Do you like it here?"

She smiles again and nods, then says something unmemorable about the school.

"Will you take a photograph of me? This was my old house."

She holds the camera while I position myself, mimicking a shot taken years before. In that photograph, I am perched on the edge of a bench leaning back against this wall; my arms are folded and my head is turned to the side. My body looks lost in the brown tweed skirt, brown sweater, brown striped shirt, brown socks and brown shoes of our uniform, and my face is closed. In that old photograph, I have receded as far from the lens as I can. This time, I look directly into the camera and smile.

30

Our car feels like a small combustible compartment as it speeds north towards Durham carrying me, my mother, Little Bit and Richard who has just flown in from Australia. It is five days after my visit to the girls' boarding school, and we are on our way to a family wedding. It is the same wedding that inspired my mother's search for a new hat months before, a search that ended in her renting a dashing purple edifice that now sits safely on the parcel shelf, while its temporary custodian does *The Daily Telegraph* crossword in the back seat. Little Bit, brought along because it is too soon to abandon her to strangers, has curled up next to my mother.

There is an undefined tension in the air. Richard is driving, despite jet lag, and his fleshy profile seems unusually menacing with the addition of a beard. The beard itself has already been a topic of family discussion: some women in the family feel it makes him seem older than his forty-seven years, while Michael has gleefully dubbed him "Captain Pugwash" after the children's cartoon character. Richard brushes off these jibes; he is used to brotherly teasing, and family dynamics rarely impede him since he lives on another continent. If anything, he relishes the heightened intensity of his short visits.

Since he is godfather to the groom, and used to live in Durham as a college student, the wedding has inspired him to make a week-long visit, combining business with pleasure. As we head north along miles of unchanging motorway, I wonder what is stirring in him. Watching Richard interact is sometimes like seeing myself from another angle; in the past, I have recognized the non-specific anger launched at my mother and the same compulsion to probe beneath the surface of things.

"Shall we stop soon for lunch?" My mother's voice floats anxiously from the back of the car. Richard is diabetic, and she is always concerned about the regularity of his meals.

We leave the motorway just outside Milton Keynes and land by chance in a village that boasts several pubs. When we settle down around a table, we are like dignitaries from three separate and volatile nations. My mother, sensing the tension, wants immediate peace at all costs, but her anxiety makes her ask foolish questions that set my brother's back up. Richard seems angry, caged, and not ready to negotiate; I am unsettled because the source and direction of the tension is unclear. As soon as possible, I leave the table and walk Little Bit up a quiet lane.

When I get back, Richard is waving impatiently from the car. We resume our imbalanced journey, stopping only once for the bathroom and a shot of espresso in cappuccino and latte form. After this refreshment, he relinquishes the wheel, but rather than dozing, as I had hoped, he gets a second wind and starts asking me questions. Although there is love between family members, there is not necessarily revelation; I am reluctant to answer questions that might probe unsympathetically into my life.

Something shifts when we leave the main road for a cross-country route to my bed and breakfast, thirty minutes outside of Durham, as if the tension had been associated with the busy roads. We slow down and appreciate the wild-looking fells, the dips and curves of landscape, and the scruffy looking heather that only weeks before would have been vibrant with colour. As our car climbs the sweeping moors of the Pennines, dodging clusters of agile sheep, we notice road markers that indicate snowfall can literally reach above one's head.

"Imagine being stranded here," my mother says.

"I was picturing backpacking across it," I reply.

"Can there really be this much snow here?" Richard adds.

We approach Stanhope by a steep hill that curves over the River Wear and passes directly in front of my lodging. This proves to be a comfortable farmhouse run, not coincidentally, by two lesbians.

"Your landlady seems nice," remarks my mother, after one of

the women welcomes us and inquires about my breakfast needs.

"I thought she was strange," counters Richard.

The room is simple and filled with welcoming dog touches: a bowl, a fleece mat, and small treats wrapped in a red bow. While I feed Little Bit, my mother frets about being late for the pre-arranged family dinner.

Back at the car, Richard is rifling through bags.

"I think I left my insulin at the pub," he confesses.

For several tense moments we keep searching, hoping to keep this information from my mother. But when Richard starts making calls to the pub, his secret is out.

"Are you sure you left it there?" Mum asks.

"Where else? I know I had it then, and it is the last place we stopped. So stupid of me!"

The woman who answers the phone at the pub has no knowledge of any bag, but we agree to stop there on our way home. In the meantime, Richard will need insulin. As he pulls the car sharply away from the kerb, he mutters contingency plans under his breath, while my mother holds *her* breath in the back seat. She taps me on the shoulder and mouths something. When I turn away, she taps me again. This time, she has scribbled a note on the edge of her newspaper.

"Mum, if you want to say something, just say it out loud."

"I think you should go with him to find the insulin," she says desperately. "I don't think he should be driving alone."

"I don't need anyone to go with me," Richard barks.

For a moment, I picture him driving madly around Durham looking for the hospital and flinging Little Bit from side to side in the back of the car. He may not want me to go with him, but there will be no peace unless I do.

We leave our tearful mother ordering wine in the comfort of a pub full of relatives, and dash off with only a soda and a bag of peanuts to keep us going.

"I know I can find the hospital from memory," Richard assures me.

"You don't think that since we are short on time you might just ask someone?"

"No, Julia. That's part of the challenge."

He whips us around the streets, pointing out favourite pubs from his university days. With only a few wrong turns, he drives triumphantly into the hospital grounds. As we wait, he regales me with stories of his student days making me realize how little I know him; there are huge sections of our lives that have run on parallel tracks with very few intersections.

When we leave to get the prescription, with fifteen minutes to spare before the pharmacy in the supermarket closes, my brother steers again from memory, giddy with the adrenalin of this time constraint. We accomplish our mission, and while he collects the insulin, I purchase a makeshift dinner of sandwiches and fruit. By the time I wend my way back to my quiet lodgings, the grassy lawn next to the farmhouse feels like a vast acreage and the murmurings of the river are sublime.

The next day, I enjoy a leisurely breakfast and a long walk while Richard and my mother take a taxi into Durham. We meet up again at their hotel, changing into our wedding clothes in less than ten minutes. Jeremy, the father of the groom, joins us for the gentle walk to the church. He looks extremely proud and quite dapper in his rented coat and tails; it is the first time he has worn such a costume.

The wedding goes off without a hitch, although the groom seems nervous and blows out his cheeks, fingers his nose, exchanges jibes with his brother, and mock-scolds his fiancée when she makes a misstep. She is held so tightly in her dress that I wonder how she can breathe. When the vows have been taken and the vicar has exhausted his attempts at humour, we leave for the reception at Durham Castle. In the great courtyard, we nibble quiches and sip champagne while the official photographer climbs nimbly into the battlements and directs us from above into various staged groupings.

It is a grand occasion made grander by dinner laid out in the Great Hall - an appropriate name given the high ceilings, huge fireplace, ponderous oil paintings and an impressive array of lances, suits of armour and coats of arms. At the far end of the room, raised on a platform, the couple and their immediate families preside at a long table. After speeches and food, the bird-like bride is still greeting people while the exhausted groom is slouched in his chair like a dissolute lord. The sheer effort involved in marrying must surely help couples remain intact.

The following day, our journey begins inauspiciously. As I draw near the hotel, my mother appears at the gate and intercepts the car.

"You're so late," she hisses. "Richard is furious. He wanted to show us around Durham. Please don't get into an argument with him. Just tell him you are sorry."

Her intervention works like expectorant; any apology dies on my lips. Even though I could easily understand Richard's frustration at having to wait, the problem lies in miscommunication, and it is hardly helped by my mother's intervention or Richard's refusal to speak. He throws bags into the car, and his face looks like an active volcano. When we tour the Cathedral, he stands alone by the outer wall, and in the centre of town, he only grudgingly shows us the shop front that used to be the family-run Doggarts Department store.

Across the bridge, over the heads of peaceful rowers, he walks paces in front of us, head down, hands clasped behind his back. Slowly, it dawns on me that this had been a significance visit for my brother, a chance perhaps to close a chapter, measure how far he had come, or simply share more of his life with family. Focused as I had been on my own survival, I had been unaware of his feelings; at the same time, he had been reticent about sharing them. It is dangerous work to guess at each other's feelings or assume we know each other's needs. If my father's death reveals anything, it is the mystery and complexity of an individual's internal world.

When we leave Durham, the balance is still tilted towards my brother and a long way from equilibrium. But when we retrieve the insulin bag from the pub, this small victory shifts the mood in our car. Richard settles back in the passenger seat, surrenders to the drive, and turns on the radio so he can listen to the Ryder Cup. The humorous commentary acts like a balm, and by the time we leave him at Michael's London home, he seems peaceful and content.

Several days later, I drive Richard to a business meeting. He has pulled a hamstring while playing in a friendly cricket match, and the injury has left him unable to press the pedals on the car. We are searching improbably for an Indian restaurant in the suburbs of Uckfield, a small village in East Sussex, and he has just brought up the subject of early sibling touch - something we remember and experience quite differently.

It is typical of our relationship that even a short visit produces such intense conversation. There is at once a similarity and distance between us that makes these conversations possible and occasionally frustrating.We share a spiritual perspective, but the language we use is different and the concepts do not always mesh.

On this occasion, as we talk about the past, I express the wish that in previous conversations on this topic he had shown more compassion.

"Do you have compassion for yourself?" was his reply.

It is a fair question. The previous evening, I had offered a hands-on healing for his pulled muscle. He had accepted, showing a surprising vulnerability. *Would I have been so open?* As I placed my hands on the top of his right thigh, close to the groin, I invoked a healing prayer for the past and for any suffering Richard experienced as boy; then I offered my forgiveness. I no longer wish to carry the past around as an unnecessary burden.

Do you have compassion for yourself? The car has become our confessional, our red cocoon on wheels, and his question makes me pay attention to my internal conversations - the "buck up, Julia" dialogue or the "blaming someone else" that feeds on a misplaced sense of injustice. He has offered me something valuable, and I will return to his words later, turning them over and touching the pointed edges the way a puppy might encounter a hedgehog or a prickly plant.

The question still hangs in the air, unanswered, when the Blue Asia restaurant comes in to view. It is right in the middle of an unpromising back road that we had assumed was residential. It is a welcome distraction. And although the building appears derelict, inside it is tastefully furnished, and we share a delicious meal of curried vegetables and chicken pasan while scooping our papadum into three different chutneys.

As we eat, we talk about the old days at Brown House, safer memories filled with unqualified pleasure; on a whim, we decide to make a detour and visit the old site. We have not been back for years, yet several things are reassuringly familiar. The shops on the main street still sell the same postcards, as well as buckets and spades for the beach, and everywhere there is hard rock candy with Selsey written all the way through it in pink sticky letters.

"Remember that fish shop run by Hilda Petts?" For some reason, we had found the name funny as children.

We are still reminiscing as we drive towards the sea, but quite suddenly I pull the car over. There on the edge of town is Terry's sweetshop – a place we visited almost every day on our bicycles, spending our precious pennies on bazooka bubble gum and sherbet dib dabs.

"Let's go inside," my brother says.

Boxes and newspapers are stacked randomly, as if the owners are in the midst of moving. The stock on the shelves is meagre and ancient, and there is an odour of neglect. But Mrs Terry is still there looking faded and worn in her flowered apron. She remembers our name and speaks respectfully of our grandmother. The encounter has a fairy tale quality, and when we drive off, I have to resist the temptation of turning back to see if the shop is still there.

The road we are on runs into the sea, but we turn right and then left past windblown fir trees. In front of us, the escalonia hedge that once marked the boundaries of Brown House now encircles many different homes. We start at the five-bar gate, the one with Brown House written in rusty letters, and walk in a large square formation guided by the hedge-line. When driveways and suburban homes interrupt our view, we peer around walls and between garages looking for anything we recognize. Richard identifies a pine tree, and we piece things together, laying out the gardens in a patchwork of guesses and combined memories.

"We didn't go to the sea very often. Do you remember? There was so much to do at Brown House."

"Imagine if we had a place like this now. We would make good use of it."

My brother must be thinking about his young sons and how they would love the space and the opportunity to play games. But their life is in another world, and I suspect this is a temporary nostalgia.

Down at the water, the tide is in lapping the wall and combing up strands of thick-ridged seaweed. A seagull perches on a metal buoy that bobs in the distance like a miniature Eiffel Tower.

"Let's go to the East Beach," my brother says.

Memories well up of old railway carriages turned into holiday homes and thick pampas grass capable of cutting small hands. Down at the seafront, the pebbled beach is lined with overturned fishing boats, and temporary stalls have been set up offering the day's catch. In an alley lined with lobster pots, we encounter a man who remembers delivering packages to Brown House when he was a young boy.

"I remember because they had a great big dog," the man laughs. "He was bigger than me."

This must be the dog that my father refers to in his diary – a Great Dane called Pluto who probably looked more ferocious than he actually was. We ask the man about the old railway carriages, and he tells us they have either been demolished or built over.

"Some people's houses actually have a railway carriage inside them for preservation," he explains.

We move on to the entrance of a walkway that leads to the Lifeboat slip lifted high on metal legs and stepping out into the water like a maritime giant. In the shed-like building, a fully equipped lifeboat dominates the room and sits ready to slide down the far ramp; the walls are covered with framed pictures and newspaper articles bearing witness to each successful launch.

"Gramy died in here, you know," Richard tells me. "She had a heart attack during a dedication ceremony."

It had happened while I was away, and the details that had reached me then were vague; it is strange how family history often comes later in snippets. Back on the walkway, we stand in silence and stare into the water that looks like an impressionist painting with tiny dots for boats.

When we return home, my mother seems tired. She has been

worrying about my brother, and the change of schedule caused by my sudden departure has unsettled her. In an outward display of her internal emotions, she floods the washing machine and waves away my offers of help; I leave her for a while with feet in water.

The following day, our wires cross over a shopping trip; when I get angry, she is reduced to a child-like state with helpless tears and stock phrases about it all being "too much." We drive to the shops with a layer of apprehension in the car like an uncomfortable second skin.

"Really, I think I am going crazy," she says.

But when I try to reassure her, she accuses me of still being angry. It does not even feel as if she is talking to me.

"I find this very stressful," she says. "What have I done? Why are you so angry at me?"

Perhaps she has slipped back in time and is speaking to my father. Her fragile emotional state is certainly reminiscent of earlier days. She is overwhelmed, confused about the weekend schedule, and nothing I say makes sense. She tells me she just feels old and is best left alone. When I try to speak, she pushes me away with hands and words.

"Oh, don't go on about it."

"I am not quite sure what you are doing," I reply.

"I am not sure either."

"Do you need anything at this moment?"

"No."

We drive home awkwardly, and a short time later, I hear her outside my bedroom door. She is sweeping up grass stains with a stiff brush that whisks the carpet like a cane. Back in the curved belly of childhood, with the warm fur of a dog pressed against my leg, Little Bit senses tension. We are holed up, lying on the bed together until I move to my desk and try writing. My mother is now scrubbing tea stains from the stairs.

The next time I hear her, she is down in the kitchen, laughing and talking with someone who has stopped in for tea. In the old days at Hillside, I would press my ear to the floor of my bedroom, cheek against the green carpet, struggling to hear the voices that drifted up from the kitchen below. If that failed, I would creep to the stairs and sit alone behind the white banister, or slide my small, angry body under the dining room sideboard. For my mother would often speak about me, worrying to friends or complaining to the cleaning lady.

After a supper of leftover potato and eggs, I join my mother in the sitting room by the fire. She tells me that her mind is not working well today; she is filled with sad memories and a feeling of great compassion for my father. Since she is reluctant to go to bed, we sit for a long while looking at old photographs and speaking about the past. Tomorrow, I will ask about happier days. I will ask about growing up in Wales, her father's passion for golf, and their holidays in Cornwall; these are all the things she loves.

31

MEMORIES TO LIVE BY

In Cornwall, my mother's memories seep in with the tide, carrying our family holidays in Crackington Haven as well as her childhood summers in Bude.

"We used to take several trains to get here from Wales,' she tells me, "with railway porters helping to load and unload our bags."

It is easy to picture her as a child, face pressed to the window of the train counting the miles. Perhaps she would have been wondering which brightly coloured guesthouse they would stay in or anticipating how she would climb the rocks and jump the waves.

Our journey to Cornwall by road in October 2008 is more prosaic, but the excitement we feel when we glimpse the sea is just as keen. We have rented a cottage within walking distance of Crackington Haven and a short drive from Bude; but, like children, we go to the first open beach we find.

Despite the season, a few surfers in wet suits still climb the waves of Widemouth Bay, appearing and disappearing like seals. Little Bit, relieved to be out of the car, shakes her body and trots happily over the dimpled sand. We follow her, faces open, relishing the crash of the waves and the whip of salted air.

After the beach, our cottage feels small: two rooms at the back for sleeping, a shared bathroom, and a front room that combines kitchen, living room and dining area. While I unpack the car and store our provisions, my mother moves to and fro on the green leather sofa, unsettled in her new surroundings and asking questions about the lights and the electric meter. It has been a long day, and we turn in early adjusting to the salty air and the sea-damp sheets.

In the first glimpse of morning, the path through the fields is wet with dew and the woods are fresh; Little Bit stops frequently for new smells. The road that leads to Crackington Haven beach is steep and lined with houses; several local dogs come out to give Little Bit the once over as we head down towards the sea.

The place has hardly changed in forty-four years. There are a few new buildings, perhaps, and a new bridge because the old one got swept away in a flood. But up on the hillside, the thatched house looks just as it did when my parents leaned against it wrapped in their beach towels. And here is the wall, cool under my inquisitive fingers, where we all sat. It is a place to rest a while.

My mother is up and dressed when I return. After toast and cereal at the small wooden table, we prepare for a morning out. We drive to Bude, stopping beyond the town where the land rises and a long stretch of green leads to the sea. My mother asks if she can walk Little Bit, but she is really walking back to the past when she played tennis here and stayed in the row of boarding houses that face the green. Down on the beach, she points out landmarks.

"There's the saltwater pool we used to swim in. Those are the rocks I would climb. I remember Joyce did a handstand right there."

"How can you remember that?"

"We used to come here every day, and all of the children would sit in front of a pulpit of sand; theology students used to put on special services. Over there, where that line of rather ugly concrete buildings now stand, was open grassland and just a few bathing huts."

She turns and points to the cliff edge where there used to be a nine-hole golf course. She tells me that her parents played golf each morning and afternoon, sending her scurrying for balls among the rocks and sand. I ask if her father played in a dog collar, but she laughs and says no. It was one of the few times he wore short sleeves, and Gubby would play in a large floppy hat.

It is strange to think of my mother as part of this other family, but in Cornwall that other life looms large. As she begins to gingerly

214

climb a line of rocks, she points out one rock in particular that appears in old family photographs. She had wanted to show me several beaches further up the coast, but the tide has moved quickly and the headland has now disappeared. Instead, we inspect the tide pools, noticing the sea moss nesting among the delicate shells and marvelling at the tenacity of mussels able to fix their blue-black bodies to the rock.

❧

My mother shares this tenacity by nature. Born, in defiance of doctor's orders, on August 2, 1922, her birth was made memorable by a water failure in the rectory; nothing but green slime came from the taps. The midwife who safely delivered her stayed on for three weeks and helped the family cope.

When she brought her lively presence and a shock of curly hair into this devout household, it was six years after the birth of my grandparents' first child and two years after my grandfather had become Rector of Cadoxton in Wales. The family had just moved into a generous-sized rectory in the neighbouring parish of Barry. Once a bustling port and coal exporter, Barry was beginning to feel the effects of coal's decline. During my grandfather's nineteen-year stint as Rector of Cadoxton and Rural Dean of three closely connected villages, he ministered to a community that was defined by poverty and unemployment.

Life in the rectory was built around my grandfather's schedule: daily morning communion and evensong, and four different services on Sundays. Gubby attended all of these services and supported her husband's work by raising money for the parish. She held regular sewing parties, twice weekly rummage sales, and an annual Church Bazaar that provided a living for the curate. Busy with these duties, she left the disciplining of children to her husband who had a knack for inspiring filial love and obedience; he most effectively expressed his displeasure through silence or, even worse, visible disappointment but took punitive action only when it was necessary. If my mother talked during church services, for instance, he would

215

sweep down mid-sermon, pluck her from the pew, and deposit her in the pulpit. Then, he would calmly resume his address as if nothing had happened.

Although duty was clearly the primary focus of their lives, it was love that had seeded my grandparents' unlikely union. Gubby had ducked one offer of marriage on board the ship that brought her from Australia, and then she had remained single for fourteen years until she eventually fell in love with my grandfather at a local tennis club. The aunt and uncle who had adopted Gubby strenuously opposed the match. For an entire year, they banned the "penniless" curate from their home. But love or stubbornness prevailed; the couple married, and the fastidious Welsh aunt summarily disinherited her charge.

In a large framed photograph that hangs halfway up the stairs of my mother's cottage, my grandmother seems wistful on her wedding day. Her face is turned slightly sideways, her mouth set in a straight line, and one of her eyes is hooded as if she cannot bring herself to look freely out. Next to her, his rugby-playing shoulders squared to the camera, William Austin Davies tilts his head. This is not a tentative pose. His chin is firm, his mouth tight in the manner of a dog holding onto a bone, and there is a steely fortitude about him that suggests he has moral certitude on his side.

Yet despite the impression that this photograph gives - which after all could be due to the careless timing of the photographer, the cruelty of the Welsh aunt, or larger events taking place in 1915 - life in London began well enough for the newlyweds. Complications set in during the second summer of married life. My grandmother gave birth to Joyce, and then promptly contracted tuberculosis. She was sent away to a sanatorium on the Norfolk coast for one year and separated from her baby of six months. From necessity, my grandfather gave up his position as Curate of All Saints Church, Battersea and took a much less profitable job nearer his wife. When Gubby finally returned to her new home, under strict instructions not to have any more children, she was a stranger to the baby-in-arms; they had to get re-acquainted during the long hours that Gubby rested, reclining in the garden on a wicker chair.

These events must have marked the young couple, setting them on a difficult financial course, testing their love and endurance, and injecting distance into my grandmother's first taste of mothering. But she was a resolute woman, devoted to her husband and his vocation, who expressed her love through fierce acts of loyalty rather than a doting, daily touch.

Her shining moment came years later when my mother was expelled from school for an unauthorized sweet shop visit. Gubby demanded they reverse the expulsion, and she confronted the startled headmistress with the question, "Have you ever known Marion to lie?" Gubby won that argument, and my mother returned to school where she was made to sit at the juniors' table for meals and walk with them each day in crocodile.

"What were intimate moments with Gubby like? What did you most love about her," I ask.

My mother hunts silently for a suitable memory.

"She loved having her hands manicured, and she could tell fortunes with tealeaves when you emptied the cup and saw how the tealeaves were laid out. She would say, 'Ooh, I see a tall dark handsome stranger'; 'Something is going to happen'; 'There is a journey.' Absolute nonsense. Daddy pooh-poohed it very much, and mother never did it when he was around."

"I don't think I was that affectionate towards my mother," she adds. "She was incredibly loyal, but there were lots of things I hated; she embarrassed us by making us play the piano in front of people. And she used to tell Daddy if we were naughty."

My mother's stories about her father carry far more warmth. She adored him and often met him on his walks back from the parishes under his care. The sight of his black cassock and hat appearing over the rise of a hill would send her running, breathless, into his arms.

"His hands were always warm," she tells me. "I wish you could have known him."

Back in the car park, she pulls me over to one corner and points to the ground.

"I lost a shilling right here. My father had given it to me, and I was devastated."

We both stare at the ground as if the shilling might still appear.

"I looked everywhere. Daddy said we would find it together."

She pauses here and smiles; her hands are thrust deep in her pockets, and her feet are splayed as a small child might stand.

"He must have had another shilling with him" she continues. "He suddenly produced one as if he had just found it. That kind of thing stays with you."

When we return to the beach in the evening, hoping the tide will be out, the water is still high at the edge of the rocks. The sun has set and surfers are leaving the cold waves when we arrive. We have consulted the tide table, but we are still one hour from the low point, and there is no way we can walk to the furthest beaches. My mother is disappointed, but she yields; memory is just out of reach.

Our week passes quickly. We visit the small grey church of Morwenstow and walk along the coast path, stopping at Stephen Hawker's shelter made entirely from driftwood. Hawker was a nineteenth century Anglican minister and poet who would sit here, high on opium, writing his poetry and gazing at a rectangle of sea. His stone bench is now covered with graffiti, but the solid walls built into the hillside are untouched, and the roof covered with mud and grass is sturdy. It is a beautiful vantage point, yet I find his view too narrow and the sides of his hut too enclosing.

One morning, rain beats down relentlessly, and we stay in the cottage and dip into the past. On rainy days in Wales, when my mother couldn't roam the beaches or explore the woods, she went into the rectory attics where there was a doll's house, a ping-pong table, and a tantalizing collection of art trunks.

"Mother never came up there," she says. "Joyce and I used to sit and read illicit books in the attic."

"What was an illicit book in those days?'

"Books like A. J. Cronin's *Hatter's Castle* with a faint little bit of sex in them, and descriptions of how babies are born. We were never told the facts of life or anything."

The attics were also the setting for theatrical presentations.

"Joyce used to write plays and we would act them out. If I forgot my lines, which I often did, Joyce would say them for me as well as acting her own part. She even wrote in parts for Edith, the maid. I can still see Edith playing a Roundhead soldier and falling through the curtain with a cake tin on her head."

There is a scrap of paper at home that announces one of these plays. To open the event and mark its solemnity, the Reverend Davis was often called on for official ribbon-cutting duties. Friends and family were also invited, and all proceeds went to a worthy cause. When their father had joked one day that the worthy cause was buying him a new hat, Joyce had indignantly corrected him. The funds, she said, were earmarked for the Lumbobo African Mission.

When the weather clears, we visit several more churches. While my mother admires the simple stone arches and towers, I appreciate the churchyards with their tipping headstones and quietly sheltering trees. On Sunday, while she attends the Harvest Festival Service at the local St. Gennys Church, I walk with Little Bit across muddy fields and down through paths of heather to the wind-blown sea. We huddle there with spray misting our faces watching the cuckoo spit fly among the grasses; our worship does not require sermons or pews.

We leave Cornwall reluctantly. On our last morning, we walk a short way along the coastal path at Crackington Haven and find a bench that looks out over the water. The early clouds have lifted, and the sea crests and falls in icy green. My mother points out the beach where Michael would play cricket; she describes how he would stand diffidently at the edges of a game until someone noticed and asked him to join in.

"And over there is the beach where I walked with your father and found the sea trees," she says, as if it had only happened a few weeks before.

The place is rife with memory; we sit together, close to the thatched house and the wall, witnessed by the roar of the sea.

32

Back home, life returns to its pattern of writing, walking, and house sitting, but the earth has shifted, and autumn has taken hold moving us down where the days are darker and the nights seem long. We speak of Cornwall with longing: What do you think the sea is like today? I wonder, is it sunny or raining? Is the tide in or out?

It is a hard autumn; the rain beats down and damp seeps into the walls of the cottage; grey skies seem to push on my head. My cousin Jeremy takes a turn for the worse, and my uncle struggles with depression brought on by complications from Addison's disease and changes in his medication. Sue, my aunt, calls. She is going away for a week and wonders if I am interested in staying with my uncle. While the depression may be temporary, she would like someone there to cook for him and keep an eye on things.

This is an opportunity. For several days, I turn the proposal over, churning like slow butter until the curd forms. Hubert is surely not used to being so vulnerable around his niece, and I am not used to caring for him compassionately. I dream about two knights, battle weary and well known to each other. They have jousted nobly, testing each other's endurance and skill. In the dream, it is time to put down weapons and commune in different ways.

Three or four clocks chime each hour at my uncle's house in Chichester, marking the time measured otherwise in books, television, and meals. Little Bit, who has come with me, dives under beds whenever a clock strikes; one afternoon, I find her shivering, in the dusty attic with cobwebs tangled in her fur.

Dust has made a home here in the carpets, window ledges,

221

cracks and corners. It is late October, and the windows are shut against the cold, refusing to open even when I pull back the white lace curtains and brush aside soft, furry piles of moth. Outside the windows, college students and families hurry past with heels click-clacking and voices going loud then soft.

With the kitchen behind and the garden to my right, I anchor myself in the dining room among the dusky furniture, family portraits, and old china. I set up my computer and prop papers on the little red bookstand Sue uses for reading. She is the heart of this house, a tall woman whose stately presence might intimidate unless you saw her playing with her grandchild or recognized the softening that life experience has wrought.

On days when it is warm enough, I sit outside where the hydrangeas have swollen to twice their normal size. Their great heads nod forward like somnambulists threatening to break their stalks. Above me, ferns poke through chimneys and the ivy creepers stretch sinewy fingers under the roof. When a gull calls, the sea is close.

Sometimes, a robin keeps me company. He cocks his head, hops along a wall and looks quizzical until I throw him a crumb or two. Then, he flits to the ground, thrusts his body over his red waistcoat, and pecks up my offering in an eager yet dignified manner. As he dances from one spot to another – the underside of a bush, the bird feeder, the dividing wall, and finally the ledge under the kitchen window- he lets me know that this is his domain.

I am merely a visitor, sitting on the hard bench and looking down the narrow garden to the flowerbed where my aunt has sprinkled some of her daughter's ashes. She told me this the last time I was here. After Evelyn's death, she bought two special roses, and as she sunk them into the earth, she added this physical reminder of her daughter's too-short life.

The last time I saw Evelyn, in the summer of 2002, she was dressed in vibrant colours, as if someone had thrown a bowl of tropical fruit and she had absorbed the yellows, reds and greens. Her eyes had seemed huge in her face, emphasized perhaps by a splash of red lipstick and two fake yellow chrysanthemums tucked behind one ear. Her newly born son, Iggy, lay in her arms - a bundle of mottled pink, eyes barely open, and fingers curling and uncurling as he slept.

We laughed a lot that afternoon; my niece, Francesca, held Iggy on her lap and let her long hair fall over his head like a wig. We took turns holding him, smiling at the strength of his tiny body and his fiece insistence on life.

"Nothing prepares you for the responsibility of a child," Evelyn had said.

A week or so later, she visited my mother's cottage with her husband, Greg, on the way to or from a music festival. They came in a battered camper van, a house on wheels, and gave Iggy a bath in my mother's tub. He had seemed miniscule - a tiny sliver of flesh waving his legs in a barrel of white porcelain.

Evelyn would have been a wonderful mother – the kind of mother who would have engaged her son's imagination and entered his dreams. As an actress, she knew how to live a bold and creative life.

In the guest room at my uncle's house, I have set up a small altar. I wonder if my cousin's spirit is hovering here; it is the same room Evelyn used when she visited with her new baby and endured the continuing sleeplessness that had plagued her in London. I wish we had been able to speak more; I wish I had known what she was thinking and feeling and what it was really like to be a new mother.

When Evelyn died cruelly in front of a train, in the early hours of one seemingly innocent morning, the shock of her death and the memory of my father made me come home. It was September, and I had seen Evelyn barely two months before. How had her vibrant life come to an end in this quiet town, this sedate city held close within its Roman walls?

As I flew home over the Atlantic, I worried that this death and its circumstances might plunge my mother into anxiety or depression. In addition to the horror of losing Evelyn, I thought it might dredge up the past. But when we gathered in a side chapel at Chichester Cathedral, my mother had been sorrowful yet calm. Her one regret, as she saw how the family coalesced into a bulwark of love and support for Evelyn, was that she had not been able to offer my father the same degree of public acknowledgement and honour.

It was a brave and shocking funeral. As I listened to my two cousins address the crowd, as my uncle read aloud from Khalil Gibran about joy and sorrow, and as Greg shared the poem-like vows he had offered to Evelyn at their wedding, it seemed impossible that she was gone. Her death was incomprehensible – a mystery that would never be solved no matter how many explanations or theories were put forward – and the harsh fact of it made me want to reach ever more intensely for the sweetness of life.

In the mornings, my uncle lies on his bed like a small boy. From the doorway I watch him curled on his side with one hand under his head and his legs pulled up into his belly. His grey flannel trousers and maroon v-necked sweater look like a prep-school uniform. On the spare bed, there are piles of books, but he ignores them and lies there with eyes open hearing the same traffic and the voices suddenly loud and then soft.

Dinner is the main meal, and my uncle takes his in the sitting room. We eat together, chair by chair, in front of the television. Sometimes, he asks questions about my graduate courses or my dissertation. If he feels animated, he shares snippets about my father and brings out photographs wondering if I have seen them.

One night, we play scrabble and when a lucky streak means that I surpass him, I feel a twinge of regret. He picks up the score sheets and studies them accusingly.

"But you told me I was winning," he exclaims.

"You were," I say. "Then I got lucky with that X placed on a triple letter score."

It was Evelyn who had urged me to know her father better, assuring me that he was fun once you got to know him. Over the years, both of his daughters had challenged Hubert with flamboyant clothes and unconventional choices, and he had shown a remarkable degree of acceptance. Later, he would remind me about an evening program he attended, when my Guru had visited England, where he and Sue both came up in darshan and bowed their heads despite possible discomfort or embarrassment. Perhaps this is what Evelyn had meant. Certainly our present wearing away of formality would have pleased her; she would have approved of the camaraderie developing over our nightly glass of wine.

My uncle gets better; his depression gradually lifts, and he once again enjoys visits to Lords and sits applauding on the sidelines when one of his grandsons' hits a ball over the boundary at a school match. He also enjoys visits from Iggy, who comes regularly, and he presides once again at the head of family gatherings. His illness will become, at least for him, a distant memory.

While my uncle recovers, my cousin Jeremy begins a rapid decline from a combination of cancer and heart disease. When my mother and I visit him in early November, we are shocked by the skeletal figure that answers our third ring at the door. Neither his sons, in the top room of the house, nor his wife, resting on the sofa, have heard us. Jeremy has made his painful way down steep stairs, clutching his intravenous drugs.

"Jeremy!" my mother exclaims.

She remembers him as a small boy - her sister's son coming to stay for holidays - and then later, as a young man expounding on one of his causes and thumping his fist at the end of our dining room table. In one photograph, taken at Brown House, Jeremy's bronzed figure towers next to my father near the swimming pool. It is Jeremy's robust physical presence, usually topped with a bushy beard, that one remembers.

He is upright still, but brittle, as if his body might snap, and terribly thin. He stands irresolute by the door, until my mother puts her hand in the small of his back and leads him up the stairs. Later, she tells me that he lay down, absolutely rigid, at one end of the bed; she had thought for a moment that it was all over. But he rallied. Erika, his wife, eased him back between the sheets, and he entertained a stream of visitors over the next few hours.

When my turn comes, his awareness is drifting between the present and the past. It is hard to believe that this is the same man who, two months previously, had stood tirelessly at his son's wedding. He smiles wanly, his head nesting in pillows and resembling a tired old owl. When I take his hand, it is relaxed, as if he were drifting into sleep.

"I am glad I took early retirement," he tells me, blinking through spectacles. His words feel prophetic - short sentences punctuated by the dry clicking of his tongue.

"Everyone will go on fine without me," he adds, with an air of satisfaction and just a hint of sadness.

We sit for a while as a breeze gently billows the curtains in the room and makes them dance. Downstairs, they are setting out plates and cups for tea.

"It is a good thing that you have come home," he pronounces deliberately, the effort of each word lending an extra weight. "Auntie is looking ten years younger. I think you will carve out a life here, and it will produce felicitous things."

I kiss his forehead and tell him, quite emphatically, that I will see him again. But when my mother and I leave the tall brick house with its rooms stacked like a child's advent calendar, we walk down the darkening lane and wonder aloud if indeed we will see him again.

Two days later, he suffers a stroke and leaves the comfort of home for an impersonal hospital room, almost paralysed on one side. We galvanize for another visit and drive down a motorway lined with bare trees. We have left home later than intended, tempers frayed by a series of misunderstandings that continue when we take the wrong exit off the motorway. Confused by the maze of criss-crossing roads, we are unable to make sense of our directions. We stop twice to ask for help, once from a kindly woman on a bicycle who calls my mother "luv" and assures us the hospital is "just over the hill there."

When at last we pull up at the jumble of pre-fabricated buildings and thread our way past ambulances through the sliding glass doors, I feel as if I have wandered onto the set of a war film. The lights are dim; several people in wheelchairs have been left in the hallway, waiting for something or someone; and the newest looking pieces of equipment are two soda machines. Near the elevators, the ceiling gapes with exposed pipes and wires like an eerie modern art exhibit, and the abundant presence of antiseptic wipe dispensers suggests germs might be lurking every twenty–five yards.

On the top floor, family members gather and wait while Jeremy receives physiotherapy from two young women. Nurses and porters shuffle past in drab uniforms, wheeling patients or carrying cups of water and bowls. There is no beauty anywhere.

When we enter his room, Jeremy's body seems limp; his head has fallen to one side, and he stares down at the bed sheets through his thick-rimmed glasses. But when I press his hand and bend to kiss him, he returns my grip with surprisingly strong fingers.

"You all look splendid," he whispers from one side of his mouth.

Erika positions us so that Jeremy must use the side of his body affected by the stroke; she was a doctor, and so she notices these things. My mother leans forward, tearfully, and her greeting is laced with pity.

"Not so much of the poor and old," Jeremy replies.

While my mother strokes his arm, people begin telling family stories in a ragged semi-circle, while I stand silent at the head of the bed. When you are dying, is it comforting to be reminded of the past? Are you measuring the value of those long gone days, or have you already shifted to another place?

Jeremy's shallow sunken chest rises and falls in the greying hospital gown, and the shoulder under my right hand feels wasted away. His eldest son feeds him grapes, peeling them first, and then offers him water through a straw. Something cracks inside me; here is a dying father, summoning up strength to whisper, "thank you" out of a half-closed mouth.

33

REST IN PEACE

A week after Jeremy's death, my mother and I sit at her kitchen table battle weary. I am in blue cotton pyjamas, and my mother is in soft velour. Her hair is a little dishevelled, and the lines under her eyes are pronounced. Death has forced subterranean feelings to the surface, and they have settled around us like mud.

My mother is a soft confusion. She wanders from room to room and project to project. Some nights, she cannot sleep, and other nights, a deep sleep leaves her groggy and disoriented. The simplest plans seem complicated, as if she were navigating a boat through swampy water.

At the kitchen table, my mother folds and refolds her napkin, pressing the material into the Formica table with all the emphasis of her strong hands. Over toast crumbs and cold tea, I surmise out loud that Jeremy's death has unsettled us both.

"I have a hard time relating to all the conversations and meetings," I tell her. "I don't really have memories of my cousin from the past. I feel as if I connected to him quietly, profoundly, during the last few weeks. So I don't really see my place in all this."

"Your place in the family?" My mother looks puzzled, but she is quick to see a larger issue from the snippets I give her.

"No, I mean my place in the rituals around his loss."

"Apparently your brother wrote a very good letter."

More napkin folding accompanies this comment. Perhaps she too is reaching for how to commemorate this death in an authentic way.

The preceding Tuesday, we had gone to my cousin's house as a gesture of support. My mother had arrived with a deep desire to comfort, but as we sat having tea with his wife and sons, Erika in particular was extremely self-possessed. It was my mother who was tearful. She had now outlived the boy she had once pushed in a stroller.

As we sat drinking cups of tea and eating cakes, my mother had rallied and began telling stories about Jeremy, emphasising the pride he felt at being a father. Submerged in my mother's rhetoric, I felt as if my voice had been subsumed in this careful re-telling of the past spoken in almost theatrical tones. It was as if I had been thrust into a play without having learned my lines.

"I don't really know what to do at all these gatherings. For a start, I didn't have a father, so I don't really relate."

There is a slight sting at the back of my eyes, but my mother launches into platitudes about the grieving family that seem disconnected to what I have just shared.

"Mum, I don't feel heard by you," I blurt out. "When I share a story or try to tell you what I am feeling, it feels as if you counter with another story but you don't really hear what I have said."

"Well, we are bound to have different views on all this," she says, after a pause. "We don't see things the same way. Sometimes, I think you condemn all men."

The comment hangs in the air, disconnected from the conversation, yet apparently following some thread inside my mother's head that I am not privy to.

I feel that my words have been terribly misconstrued. My stripped down comment had been pregnant with unexpressed emotion. I uncross my arms, attempt a wan smile, but feel the stab that accompanies her words. The mischaracterization is a small dagger, thrust under my defences into an exposed and tender part; I do not hold all men accountable for my father's death.

"What are you talking about? Give me an example."

"Well, I don't really know what you think," she says at last, as if I am a mystery.

"Mum, what is the connection between this and my sharing what I felt about my cousin's death?"

"I don't really know," she answers. "I feel confused."

"Well, is there something you would like to ask me? Is there anything you want to know about my beliefs?"

My hands are open in a gesture of invitation. But my mother does not avail herself of this. In the moment where I see possibility for connection, she backs off.

"Let's just carry on shall we?" She wants an end to the conversation.

"Well, if you are not interested in learning more about me, then I would ask that you don't make these false general statements."

A half-hour later, she comes to my room and puts her hand on my shoulder. She tells me she is sorry.

"I do not know what is the matter with me," she says. "I am being an old fool."

Jeremy's funeral is on the first day of December. The air is bright; the sun plays on the small boats bobbing in Portsmouth Harbour; and the brown granite walls of the crematorium are sharply, starkly outlined. My mother and sister-in-law have just picked me up at the railway station, where I have arrived from spending the weekend with an old school friend. In the back seat of Mum's car, I wriggle out of my jeans and fleece and into funeral clothes.

My mother drives to the crematorium in stop-start fashion, as if gears were an afterthought and lane-changes her privilege alone. Caroline is navigator, and I am assistant-driver from the back seat, checking traffic flow and alerting my mother to imminent danger. Each turn is a collaborative decision and each roundabout an over-choreographed confusion. We turn gratefully into the crematorium on the heels of a sleek black hearse.

Clusters of relatives stand in the windswept parking lot, kissing cheeks and making small talk. They are the same faces from the wedding two months before. At the side of the building, my mother mistakenly thinks the women's restroom is occupied; she surrenders her usual sense of boundaries and tries the men's, while Caroline and I wait patiently outside the ladies only to discover no one is there.

Our group is ushered towards a waiting room that is bare except for a water dispenser and green worsted sofa seats that line each wall. It is a way station, an anonymous room that fills and empties with mourners day after day, and we shuffle nervously, until a man in a dark suit herds us into the chapel. On the far wall, empty hooks that usually support a cross show that Jeremy's request for no religious icons has been scrupulously respected.

Pachabell's Canon pipes into the room and the service begins. Three people pay tribute to him. The first is a long–time friend who describes Jeremy's passion for social justice. He tells a funny, touching story of their student days when they had lived off pilchards in every conceivable combination because they were cheap, available and nutritious. The second speaker sketches my cousin's professional life, his wide and varied knowledge, his penchant for vigorous debate, and his passion for motorbikes and all mechanical things. The final speaker reveals the pleasures of having had my cousin as a neighbour for thirty years. She conjures him up on the back patio, working in the garden or playing with his sons, when his laughter would easily cover the distance between their two homes.

In front of me, Ann's shoulders are hunched and vulnerable in a beige overcoat. She is mourning a brother, and their shared early world is not represented here. A person can mean so many different things to different people; how do we best remember him?

At the crematorium in Leatherhead, where my father's body was taken and burned, there is barely any record of his death. Supposedly, his name is written in the Book of Remembrance that is housed in a small chapel covered with memorial plaques.

On the day that my mother and I visit the crematorium, the chapel is already closed. We have parked our car in the wrong place and wasted precious minutes walking through the spacious grounds.

"How come you didn't know which was the right door?" I ask.

Unreasonable anger keeps other, stronger feelings at bay. Everywhere I look, there are memorials of one kind or another, but none that were here forty years before.

"How did you decide what to do?" I ask.

"I was sent lots of forms to fill out. I didn't know what I wanted," my mother replies.

With no money for fancy headstones, plaques, or benches my mother had opted for a rose with a two-year shelf life. She remembers it being packed into a crowded garden, but when she came back some years later, it had gone. The existing roses are in a beautiful walled garden with black wrought-iron gates, but my mother is not even sure if this is the same place.

"Why is there so much vagueness about something so important?"

"It was arranged by other people," she tells me in a faltering voice. "I just did what I was told."

"Why didn't you get more support? Why didn't someone else pay for a headstone?"

She struggles to remember.

"No one talked about him," she finally says, "and I suppose I was too afraid to speak up."

We walk in silence, stopping to look at a rose bed commemorating children - outrageous, early deaths marked by stuffed bears, angel statues and other inadequate mementos.

"I never liked the idea of the crematorium," my mother says. "Your father was always with us."

The year after Evelyn died, I visited Zari in Colorado on the thirty-eighth anniversary of my father's death. I asked if it was possible to commune with him even though he was dead.

When the session began, Zari summoned my father's presence and asked questions to verify who he was. At the time, the things he mentioned did not mean much: a memory of Paris, something about the left side of his body, a reference to musicals, and a statement about his love of wide-open spaces. But later, my mother helped make sense of these comments. They had gone to Paris on the last day of their honeymoon; he had partially lost his hearing and broken one of his legs during a football game; the two of them loved attending musicals.

"Your father is here," Zari told me. "See if you can feel him."

There was a sensation in my body - a trembling energy that felt pleasant and excitable.

233

"Why did he do it?"

She repeated the question, using 'you' instead of 'he' as if she was holding a conversation with someone in the room. Then she translated his reply.

"He could not deal with things. He wanted to go to sleep and not wake up. He wanted peace. He felt as if an eye was following him on the earth. It got worse when he was twenty-nine."

As she sent him relief in the form of white light, I felt great waves of emotion: a weight was leaving my chest.

"He is sorry he was not there to take you to ballet or watch you read. He is proud of you and what you have done."

"What can I offer Mum from you?" I asked.

He directed me to find her a shawl - a soft green shawl for comfort, so that she did not feel so alone.

Months later, the shawl appeared in a gift shop in Illinois. It was a perfect, soft green and everything in me said this was the one. But there was a thread pulled, and I hesitated about buying it. An intuitive friend suggested that I buy the shawl and ask my father about the significance of the pulled thread.

Alone in my meditation room, I held the shawl and closed my eyes. I asked to be open to receiving a message from my father, and then I sat still and listened. Clearly, with silent words, I felt him communicate, and I wrote down a poem that was addressed to my mother.

At the end of that year, I brought the shawl and the poem on a family trip to Australia. We had come to see Richard, his wife, and their two sons; they had embarked on a new business venture and were opening a luxury boutique hotel and conference site. My brother was in his element as a proud father and an excited entrepreneur; although their house was not quite ready to receive us, he made sure we were lodged in a beautiful rental property right on the sea.

My mother loved being able to walk along the beach, and one afternoon, I gave her the shawl and the poem just as she was setting out. Much later, she came to me with tears in her eyes. She had sat for hours by the sea, the shawl wrapped around her shoulders, and had felt my father's gentle, loving presence by her side.

34

My mother has saved so many letters – the ones from my father during their courtship, a few that he wrote to Michael, and every letter each of her three children has written from their respective boarding schools. She seems to have saved every letter but one.

"How come you didn't keep the suicide note?"

"I was in shock. Your father had been upbeat that day. He had gone to get decorating supplies. As the day crept on and he did not return, I began to worry. But I had the three of you to consider. I couldn't just leave you."

"What did the note say? Isn't it seared into your memory?"

"It was all so long ago; I really don't remember. I threw it away."

Nine days before he went to the edge of the world and did not come back, my father wrote to Michael at boarding school. He mentioned a recent visit where the two of them had tobogganed together, and he described the decorating he and Mum were doing at home. Michael had apparently chosen new wallpaper for his bedroom, and Dad was sure it was going to look nice. Before he signed off, he told Michael that his little sister, Julia, sent a big kiss.

Five days later, he wrote again. Just four days before his death, he described an afternoon of family gardening. He told Michael he was particularly pleased the cultivator was working since it had been in storage all winter. He also gave a decorating update: he and Mummy had stayed up late. They had finished wallpapering the bathroom, and he had put in half of the new yellow bathroom tiles. On Monday, he would begin Michael's room. He knows they must hurry, since they only had two weeks to get it done before the end of term.

Only he doesn't finish that project. A few days later, he goes out to buy more decorating supplies, and he does not come back. Sometimes, I wonder if he wrote the letter first and carried it with him. Or did he write it there, once he had taken the pills and was sitting looking at photographs of his three children? Was he lonely? Was he afraid? What were his last thoughts as he began to feel the effect of the pills and his conscious awareness of the world was slipping away?

꧂

My father chose to end his life not too far from a place we used to call the edge of the world. In my memory or imagination, the edge of the world was a semi-circular parking lot covered with fallen leaves. There were high banks and tree roots; it felt like the inside of a bomb crater, smoothed out by devastation and open to the sky.

We drove there last summer, my mother and I, making a pilgrimage to the small, chalk quarry tucked neatly into the Surrey countryside. We passed the golf club where I used to play tennis and squash as a child, and we wound our way up a series of country lanes. The day was sunny, and the trees that arched over the road were backlit, turning the leaves an emerald green.

On the back seat of the car were two red roses, freshly picked from my mother's garden and almost the colour of merlot. As we made turns according to instinct and my mother's long ago memory, she was surprised at the number of houses slotted along the roads. Since my father passed this way, there had been a steady encroachment of people, edging out woodland and field with their large houses and manicured lawns; my father's oasis of quiet may have been compromised.

Quite suddenly, we broke free of the houses; the car swept down a long hill between fields, and we made a steady climb towards a wooded area lined with a dark canopy of yew. A flash of orange stole my attention. I stopped the car and backed up. A slender fox, white blazed belly slinking low, skirted the edge of a field. He was watching a group of ewes with their lambs, nosing the air, and eying up his chances.

Our car startled him. He lifted his head, turned, hesitated and then vanished back among the trees leaving a musty scent behind him. I pushed on, turning the nose of the car uphill until my mother pointed to a small, semi-circle of white in a tangle of overturned trees and nettle.

"It's there," she told me. "I'm sure of it."

We parked at the side of the road in a slight clearing. In silence, she handed me one of the roses and kept the other. We held them in both hands like a prayer.

The quarry had been claimed by nature. The white chalk made a soft, crumbling backdrop; trees offered their roots as a woven shelter; and there was birdsong in the air. My mother stood softly in the tangle of green with her head lifted slightly, as if listening, and her body surrendered and calm. I walked around her and climbed onto a chalky ledge where I crouched, breathing the rich earthy peace of the place. There were no ghosts here.

She placed her rose under a small tree; I lay mine in an alcove where it sat like velvet against the white chalk. When she returned to the car with small, firm steps, I lingered, able to feel the place more distinctly now that she had gone.

I ran my hands over the chalk and prised off one of the soft pieces. It fit neatly into the palm of my hand, and I closed my fingers into a fist. I wondered if my father had touched this same piece of chalk, if he had sat where I was sitting, and if he too felt the peace of this place.

35

All day, I have sudden, unaccountable rushes of love for my mother. It begins when we examine signs of a mouse visitation. We note the tiny teeth marks in tomatoes and the shavings of apple heaped in a pile at the edge of the fruit bowl. The mouse seems to have run in place on the surface of an apple, churning up the peel as if he had little spikes on his feet. I am ready to pitch everything. The bowl is poised over the trash when my mother swoops in and saves a pristine green apple.

"I am going to eat my apple," she declares.

Suddenly we laugh. We discuss the nerve of this particular mouse.

"He ran right past my spray bottle of peppermint oil and water, my humane mouse deterrent," I say. "It is written right there on the side of the bottle: humane mouse deterrent."

"Perhaps he could not read," she replies.

I stalk the kitchen cabinets with a flashlight searching for dark signs of our visitor. I shine it at my mother, and she laughs weakly. I suddenly realize I have sliced my bread with the knife that our little friend probably scampered over - too late to undo that one. We agree that we will keep apples and tomatoes in the fridge from now on.

While I eat more toast and drink my tea, Mum sits at the table wrapping small packages of homemade fudge. She keeps up a running commentary.

"This is just sugar really."

"All the pieces are going to crumble."

"Would *you* eat this if I gave it to you?"

She bunches the green crepe paper and turns a package in her hand, as if she is ten years old with a challenging craft project.

"Oh well," she says, "I suppose it is like having a spoonful of sugar in coffee, right? I didn't know what else to give them." She, regrets the fact that her mincemeat is only a day old and has not yet soaked up the brandy.

The 'them' in question are a group of women she plays tennis with on a regular basis. For my mother still finds pleasure in a great many things.

"I am past my sell-by date," she likes to say, as she rubs her painful knees or lies down for an afternoon rest, but her vibrant life belies her words.

I used to believe that if I was vigilant, if I did all the right things, then my mother would not die. And she hasn't. She has stayed with us, strong and resilient, for as long as we have needed her. My mother's love has overridden my father's short existence and softened his implied statement about the insufficiency and cruelty of life.

❧

The body of a fox lies by the side of the road leading in to the village; someone has placed him there to be safe from the traffic. His soft, amber beauty moves me. He is young, and the brush of his tail sweeps up against the dark fur on his back legs. His gentle neck is thrown back slightly in release to death, and a thin trickle of blood runs from the side of his mouth. I touch him, and death settles in my body. With his mouth open, it seems as if he is calling his last sound upon the earth.

Today, I listened to my father's voice transposed from an old record - a heavy aluminium disc pre-45s, recorded in Harrods Department Store some time in the 1930s. My aunt, Pat, had sent it when she heard that I was tracing my father's story.

The voice record was such ancient technology it was incompatible with our current systems. But I had found an eccentric inventor in Bath who had machinery that could play the record with a homemade wooden needle. I drove down there, and he transposed the record, via computer, onto a regular disc. When I first heard my father's voice, it was through two giant speakers, and I was sitting on an old sofa surrounded by piles of paper and bits of odd machinery in this man's house.

*"Hello Mummy and Daddy. I'm going to recite to you.
It's Peter Doggart."*

The voice is high-pitched; the little boy rolls his 'r' sounds and annunciates, as if he is afraid of not being understood. He recites *The Gardener* by Robert Louis Stevenson, and I imagine him in a tweed jacket with leather patches on the elbows even though he is only eight or nine years old.

The fox fits in a wheelbarrow, his body stiffening although his ears are soft. I carry him into the woods and dig a shallow grave under a holly bush. While his cheek cradles the earth, I cover him with soil and rotting leaves, starting at his back and moving slowly to his head with its protruding ear, slack mouth and perfect white teeth.

My story has run its course, owning me and releasing me like the little boy in the poem - the child who mourns that the gardener will not play with him and lets summer slide to winter with never a word or a smile. Faintly in my head, the last sounds of my father's voice at the end of the poem ring out:

"Goodbye everyone," he calls, "goodbye."

A small bower of twigs for protection, a prayer, and it is done. The soft mound lies there still, curved under the holly like a child's tomb. We must trust the dead. We must set our fierce love free.

NOTES ON THE TEXT

In this memoir, I have changed or omitted some of the names to respect the privacy of individuals. The events and memories are all true.

ABOUT THE AUTHOR

Julia Doggart was born in Surrey, England in 1963. She left England in 1982 and lived abroad for many years. After graduate studies at the University of Wisconsin-Madison, she returned to England where she now lives. This is her first book.

Lightning Source UK Ltd.
Milton Keynes UK
UKHW022216030321
379729UK00007B/266